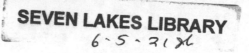
COMPETITIVE

BIDDING

IN

MODERN BRIDGE

by Edgar Kaplan

♠ ♡ ◇ ♣ ♠ ♡ ◇ ♣ ♠ ♡ ◇ ♣

Melvin Powers
Wilshire Book Company

12015 Sherman Road, No. Hollywood, CA 91605

Copyright © 1965
Fleet Publishing Corporation

All Rights Reserved

Library of Congress Catalog Card Number: 65–17415

Printed in the United States of America

ISBN 0-87980-347-9

PREFACE

♠   ♡   ◇   ♣

So far as I know, this is the first full-length treatment of competitive, defensive bidding—that is, of auctions which are started by an enemy opening bid. Most "complete" bridge books devote a casual chapter or two to doubles and overcalls, but their hearts belong to the opening bidder and responder. The defending side is neglected; they are the bridge authority's step-children.

Yet, unless you are one of the great card-holders of all time, *one-half* of your auctions begin with an opponent's opening. And competitive bidding is actually of greater importance than is strictly offensive bidding. When you go down in an uncontested auction, the set is likely to be 50 or 100 points; in competitive auctions, the penalties are often ten times as large. When you reach a foolish contract with the opponents silent, you lose the part score or game you could have made, but if you remain silent and let the enemy make a contract when you could have out-bid them, you lose twice as much—your score *plus* theirs. In every form of bridge, from a friendly home game to a top flight tournament, it is competitive bidding which makes the consistent winner.

In this book, I have tried to present a complete system of defensive bidding: first, a new and sound foundation of bids and responses to allow safe and accurate search for your own contract; second, a preemptive style with which to bedevil the·opponents; third, tools and tactics for use against special enemy opening bids; finally, an examination and evaluation of many new competitive conventions.

Over the past fifteen years, there has been a revolution in the expert approach to competitive bidding. It is high time that you benefitted from it. Whether you play bridge for fun, money, or masterpoints, this modern style will help you get more out of the game.

E. K.
New York, 1965

CONTENTS

♠ ♡ ♢ ♣

PREFACE   3

1. DEFENSIVE BIDDING   11
   Bidding After an Enemy Opening   11
     What Is the Risk?   11
     What Can Be Gained?   12
     Quiz   13
   Old-Fashioned Defensive Bidding   16
     Doubles and Overcalls   16
     The Trouble with Old-Fashioned Bidding   18
   Weak Jump Overcalls   20
     What Can You Gain?   20
     Negative Inferences from Failure to Jump   23
   Modern Defensive Bidding   24
     Jump Overcall, Takeout Double, Simple Overcall   24
     Examples   25

2. THE TAKEOUT DOUBLE   27
   Requirements for Double   27
     When Is Double for Takeout?   27
     Distributional Requirements   28
     Point Count Requirements   29
     Quiz   30

Responding to Takeout Double 31
  Penalty Pass 32
  Negative or Positive Response 32
  Counting Points as Responder 33
  Quiz 33
  Cue-bid Response 35
  Free Response 37
    At the one-level 37
    Jump responses 38
    At higher levels 38
    Examples 39
  Notrump Responses 40
Doubler's Rebid 42
  Over Minimum Reply 42
  Over Positive Reply 45
  Quiz 45
Two-Suit Doubles 46
  Requirements 47
  Responses 47
  Free Responses 48
Takeout Doubles by Passed Hand 49

3. THE OVERCALL   50
When to Overcall 50
  Trump Value of Suits 51
  Quick Tricks 52
  Vulnerability 54
  Two-Suiters 54
Responding to Overcalls 56
  Raising an Overcall 56
  Jump Raises 57
  Notrump Responses 58
  New Suit Responses 59
  After Two-Level Overcalls 61
  Quiz 62
The Immediate Cue-Bid 63
  Requirements 63
  Responses 63
  Freak Two-Suiters 65

The One-Notrump Overcall   65
   Requirements   65
   Responses   66
   Stayman Convention   67

4. THE WEAK JUMP OVERCALL   68
   When to Jump   68
      Jump or Simple Overcall?   69
      Quiz   70
      Strength Required   72
   Responding to Jump Overcall   72
      Don't   72
      Going to Game   73
      Sacrificing   75
      Raising   78
   Higher Jump Overcalls   79
      Double-Jump Overcalls   80
      Triple-Jump Overcalls   81
   Unusual Notrump Overcall   81
      When an Overcall Is Unusual   82
      Requirements   83
      Responding to the Unusual Notrump   84
         Preference   84
         Jump Response   85
         Examples   86
      A Warning   88

5. TRAPPING AND BALANCING   90
   Trapping   90
      Trap Pass   90
      When Not to Double   91
      Delayed Double   92
   Reopening the Auction   93
      Reopening Doubles   94
         Requirements   94
         Examples   94
         Responses   95
         Quiz   95

Reopening Overcalls 96
Reopening Jump Overcalls 97
Reopening One Notrump Overcalls 98
Passing Instead of Reopening 98
Balancing Later in the Auction 100
Balancing Overcalls 100
Balancing Doubles 101
Quiz 102
Responding to Balancing Bids 103
Responding to Balancing Overcalls 104
Responding to Balancing Doubles 105
When Not to Balance 106
Misfit Auctions 106
After One Notrump Response 107

6. OVER PREEMPTIVE OPENINGS   109
Passing Over Preempts 110
Takeout Double Over Preempts 110
Point Count Requirements 110
Distributional Requirements 111
Quiz 112
Responding to Partner's Double 113
Penalty Pass 113
Simple and Jump Responses 115
Cue-bid Responses 117
Quiz 118
Overcalling Over Preempts 119
Requirements 119
Jumps to Game 121
Immediate Cue-bid 121
Balancing After Preemptive Opening 122
Balancing Double 123
Balancing Overcall 124
Quiz 124
Against Higher Preemptive Openings 125
Doubles and Overcalls 126

Defense Against Weak Two-Bids 127
Two Diamond, Two Heart Openings 127
Two Spade Openings 128
Two Notrump Overcall 128
The Fishbein Convention 128

7. OVER ONE-NOTRUMP
OPENING BIDS   131
Against 16–18 Point Notrump Openings 133
Penalty Double 133
Over Partner's Double 135
The Overcall 136
Quiz 138
After Partner's Overcall 139
The Landy Convention 140
Responding to Landy 141
In the Balance Position 143
Against 12–14 Notrump Openings 144
The Double 144
After Partner Doubler 146
The Overcall 147
Quiz 148
Response to Partner's Overcall 148
The Landy Convention 149
Response to Landy 149
In the Balance Position 151
Natural Two-Club Overall 153

8. PENALTY DOUBLES   154
Doubling Part Scores 155
Doubling Games 157
Doubling by Ear 158
Doubling Slams 160
Lead-Directing Doubles 162
Examples 162
Doubling Three Notrump 164
When Your Side Has Been Silent 164
When You Have Been in the Auction 165

9. NEW IDEAS IN COMPETITIVE BIDDING   167

The Responsive Double   167
Requirements   168
Development of the Auction   169
After Partner Overcalls   170
Evaluation   171
The Michaels Cue-Bid   172
Distribution and Strength Required   173
Responding to Michaels Cue-Bid   174
Evaluation   175
The Ripstra Convention   176
Requirements   176
Responses   177
Evaluation   177
Astro over Notrump Openings   179
Distribution, Strength Required   179
Responding to Astro   180
Further Development of the Auction   181
Evaluation   183
Weiss over Preemptive Openings   185
Double, Takeout, or Pass   185
Evaluation   186
Cue-Bid Responses to Overcalls   187
The General-Purpose Cue-Bid   187
Evaluation   188
Roman Jump Overcalls   189
Requirements   189
Evaluation   190
Two-Suited Simple Overcalls   191

1

DEFENSIVE BIDDING

♠ ♡ ◇ ♣

BIDDING AFTER AN ENEMY OPENING

Any treatment of defensive bidding should start with this warning: *it is extremely dangerous to enter the auction over an opponent's opening bid.*

What Is the Risk?

The biggest penalties in bridge—the sets that run into four figures—come from business doubles of overcalls or of responses to takeout doubles. Primarily, this is because almost all intervening calls are overbids. A player who bids two diamonds over an enemy one-spade opening contracts to take 8 tricks, but he seldom can do so with his own hand—he is gambling on finding partner with some useful cards. And when he loses this gamble he goes down, often quite a lot, and doubled.

Of course, the opening bid is usually an overbid also—not many hands worth only a one-bid will take the promised seven tricks opposite a complete bust. But the opening bid is a great deal safer than an overcall, because it cannot be doubled for penalties as readily. Virtually every bidding system in the world has abandoned the business double of an opening suit bid, since neither opponent can double it effectively in complete ignorance of the quality of his partner's hand. In contrast, any intervening action over an opening bid is easy to punish; opener has guaranteed specific values, and responder can base his double on 26, not 13 cards.

What Can Be Gained?

However, "safety first" is not a winning policy at contract bridge. You must count not only what you can lose but also what you stand to gain by defensive bidding. And the rewards may be very great indeed. *First,* the hand may belong to your side despite an opponent's opening; you will occasionally be able to bid and make a game, when responder is weak and the opening a minimum, and often you can compete effectively for a part score. *Second,* you may lay the groundwork for a successful sacrifice bid; even if the hand belongs to the opponents, you may lose less playing it yourself. *Third,* by bidding you may help partner find an effective defense when the opponents buy the contract. *Fourth,* but nearly first in importance, you may make life a lot harder for your opponents; by using up their bidding room with bids of your own, you crowd the auction and often force them to guess at their correct contract, while they could have investigated carefully had you passed.

Therefore, fear of a sizable penalty should not automatically keep you out of the auction. Good defensive bidding is a process of weighing possible loss against possible profit. In deciding what you have to gain by bidding, ask yourself these four questions:

(1) Are you rich enough in high cards to believe that your side may have more points than opener's?

(2) Do you have such freakish distribution that even if

the opponents "own" the hand, you may have a cheap sacrifice?

(3) Do you strongly desire partner to lead your suit on defense?

(4) How much of the opponents' bidding space will you take away if you come into the auction?

In gauging what the cost of bidding may be, the key questions are concerned with the trump suit, for if you can win enough trump tricks, no set—even a large one—will be a true loss. The opponents will always have been able to make as many, or more, points playing the hand at their own contract. So,

(1) Do you have a long, solid suit which will take four or five trump tricks even opposite a singleton in partner's hand?

(2) Can you offer partner a choice of two or three different trump suits, so that a fit in any one will provide safety?

Quiz

Let us weigh some example hands on these scales. Suppose your right-hand opponent opens with one club. Will it pay, on balance, to enter the auction with:

(a) ♠ K Q 10 9 x x   ♡ x x   ◊ J 10 x x   ♣ x
(b) ♠ x x   ♡ A J x x x   ◊ A K J   ♣ K x x
(c) ♠ x x x   ♡ A Q   ◊ A x x x   ♣ Q J x x
(d) ♠ Q x   ♡ K x   ◊ J 9 x x x x   ♣ A J x
(e) ♠ J x x x   ♡ A Q x x   ◊ K J x x   ♣ x

Examining these one by one, we find:

(a) ♠ K Q 10 9 x x   ♡ x x   ◊ J 10 x x   ♣ x

Holding only six high-card points, you have every reason to believe that the hand belongs to the opponents. But you have freakish enough distribution to make a profitable sacrifice seem likely (and so little defense that the opponents can probably make whatever they bid). You surely want partner to lead spades on defense. And a spade bid over one club cuts away quite a lot of bidding space—if partner can raise, you may be able to destroy enemy communications. So there is a good deal to gain by bidding.

And it is safe to bid, for you will win four or five trump tricks regardless of partner's holding. You can be set, but the opponents will beat you with aces and kings, not with small trumps; with all this power, the opponents could score more points by bidding than by doubling.

Clearly, you should enter the auction, for the profit may be great and the risk is negligible.

(b) ♠ x x   ♡ A J x x x   ◇ A K J   ♣ K x x

Here, the hand is quite likely to belong to your side, for, with 16 high-card points, you probably are stronger than opener. However, you certainly do not want to suggest a sacrifice against an enemy contract, as you have even distribution and great defensive strength. You do not necessarily want a heart lead from partner. A bid will interfere with the opponents' auction only slightly. Still, you stand to gain a considerable amount by bidding, since 9 or 10 points in partner's hand may produce game at hearts or notrump.

It is dangerous to bid, though. You have no real choice of suits to offer partner, and a heart contract will be disastrous if partner is short (as he will be if you are doubled). Your high cards guarantee against a four- or five-trick set, but even a small penalty will be a total loss—the opponents cannot make a high contract of their own; they will beat you with trump tricks, not with aces and kings.

So it is less clear-cut to bid with this example than with the first one. You *should* bid, for bright game prospects outweigh all danger, but you are taking your life in your hands.

(c) ♠ x x x ♡ A Q ◇ A x x x ♣ Q J x x

Since you have only 13 points, there is a less than even chance that your side owns the hand (opener probably has at least as much as you have, and may well have more). Your flat distribution and strong defense rule out sacrifice bidding. You do not wish to direct an opening lead. No action you can take will use up much bidding room. So there is hardly anything to gain.

And there is very little safety either. You have no good trump suit of your own, and have adequate support for only one of the three unbid suits. Therefore, it is wrong to enter the auction; just pass.

(d) ♠ Q x ♡ K x ◇ J 9 x x x x ♣ A J x

It is possible that your side can make more than the enemy can, but the odds are against it, particularly since your low-ranking suit puts you in poor competitive position. Sacrifice bidding is most unattractive, despite the long suit, for your distribution is not freakish (most of the opponents' high cards will cash) and you have enough defense to hope to defeat a game contract. You certainly do *not* want a diamond lead from partner. A diamond bid will use up no bidding space and can hardly impede the opponents at all. You can gain by bidding only if partner has a specific hand: a fit in diamonds with enough strength to push the opponents too high, but not enough to warrant his entering the auction independently.

You must weigh this small chance for a profit against a hefty risk. Your suit, although long, is shabby; it provides no insurance against disaster if you are doubled. And you have scant support for any run-out if the axe falls.

Therefore, pass. If your six-card suit were in spades instead of diamonds, the increased chance of owning the hand and the greater preemptive value of competition would tip the scales in favor of bidding despite the danger.

(e) ♠ J x x x ♡ A Q x x ◊ K J x x ♣ x

Here again you have fewer points than opener. But your excellent support for the major suits puts you in strong competitive position—you may easily be able to outbid the opponents for a part-score, and even a game is in view if partner is fairly strong. A paying sacrifice may be available if partner's hand is unbalanced, for your singleton club is promising. You do not want to direct a lead, and no sensible action has much preemptive value. Still, there is a lot to gain.

You do not have a strong suit of your own. However, you have a snug harbor in any one of the three unbid suits in which partner has length. It is quite safe to bid.

Clearly, then, you should enter the auction. This three-suited pattern, short in opener's suit, rates very high on both scales—gain and safety. There is a fine chance either to own the hand or to find a cheap sacrifice. And there is little chance of a disastrous penalty, for a good trump suit is almost always available.

So far, we have concerned ourselves solely with *whether* to bid or not. Let us turn now to *what* to bid.

OLD-FASHIONED DEFENSIVE BIDDING

Doubles and Overcalls

Defensive bidding must cover a range of strength much wider than that of the opening bid. Opening bids are based on at least moderately strong hands, but it is highly desirable, as we have seen, to enter the auction defensively with many weak, distributional hands which would not be even considered for an opening. Any well worked-out system must distinguish between the hands of opening-bid strength or greater, which give promise of a possible game, and the weaker hands which are worth bidding only in order to impede the enemy or to find a sacrifice. Fortunately, there are many different defensive actions available: *the simple overcall, the jump overcall, the double jump overcall, the one-notrump overcall, the cue-bid,* and *the takeout double.*

The simple overcall and the takeout double are by far the most common actions, and the heart of old-fashioned defensive bidding lies in the distinction between them. The overcall is used to describe the weaker range of hands —those with good distributional values but lacking the high-card content for an opening bid. The takeout double is used for an overwhelming majority of hands in the strong range, largely to tell partner, "Don't be intimidated by the opening bid; I have that much and maybe more." A good suit can be shown later, over the forced response; first the takeout double must be made in order to show strength.

With rare, specific weak hands, the ones that would have been opened with three-bids, the preemptive double jump overcall is employed instead of the simple overcall. And with rare, specific strong hands, the one-notrump overcall ("I would have opened with one notrump"), the cue-bid ("I would have opened with a two-bid"), or the jump over-call ("I have a very powerful hand with a long, semi-solid suit") can be used in place of the takeout double. But these are exceptional, once-in-a-blue-moon, bids. Virtually the whole workload is carried by the simple overcall and the takeout double.

Examples

Let us consider how the examples previously given would be handled with old-fashioned defensive bidding methods.

Hand (a) in the earlier examples:

♠ K Q 10 9 x x   ♡ x x   ◊ J 10 x x   ♣ x

is a typical one-spade overcall—weakness in high cards compensated by excellent distribution.

Hand (b):

♠ x x   ♡ A J x x x   ◇ A K J   ♣ K x x

is a normal take-out double—great high-card strength and bright game prospects. The *method* of entering the auction —double or overcall—clearly indicates to partner the *motive* for entering the auction—hoping to buy the contract or trying to impede the opponents.

But what about hand (e)?

♠ J x x x   ♡ A Q x x   ◇ K J x x   ♣ x

This hand is really in the weak, distributional class, but obviously it is better suited to a takeout double than to an overcall. You do not want to bid a suit of your own; you want to double and force partner to name *his* best suit.

The Trouble with Old-Fashioned Bidding

Now, right here you can see the great flaw in classical defensive bidding. The takeout double describes strength without regard to distribution. But since it forces partner to bid a suit, the inherent meaning of a takeout double is "I have the sort of hand which will play best in partner's longest unbid suit." To have it say, instead, "I have a strong hand," is to give it a meaning every bit as artificial as the Italian one-club opening which announces not clubs, but 17 points or more in high cards. And whenever you give an artificial meaning to a bid, you pay a heavy price.

Part of this price is paid in getting up one level higher before bidding your suit. If you double a one-club opening with:

♠ x x   ♡ A J x x x   ◇ A K J   ♣ K x x

and partner responds one spade, you must bid two hearts. And this is frightfully dangerous. Even one heart is far from safe opposite a worthless hand. It seems unfair, but it is just when you are doubled and need help that dummy comes down with none. After all, there are only 40 points in the deck.

Another part of the price is paid in confusion in responding to takeout doubles, particularly when opener's partner raises preemptively over the double.

Suppose the auction has gone:

OPENER	PARTNER	RESPONDER	YOU
1 ♣	Double	3 ♣	?

What do you bid with:

♠ Q 10 x x x   ♡ K x   ◊ Q x x   ♣ x x x ?

You had better pass if partner holds the example double above, for you are very likely down at three spades and are headed for disaster if partner takes out to four hearts.

But if partner has doubled with:

♠ J x x x   ♡ A Q x x   ◊ K J x x   ♣ x

you want to bid three spades, which will make easily while the opponents can probably make three clubs. And if partner holds the king of spades instead of the jack, you would miss a game by passing.

Nowadays, more and more of your opponents are learning the value of taking preemptive action over your takeout doubles. And as long as the double is artificial, showing strength instead of distribution, you will be put to an impossible guess whenever they do.

Yet if you decide to have your defensive bidding describe your distribution—to overcall whenever you have a distinct preference for a trump suit and to double only when you can support all unbid suits, how can partner tell whether you have 6 points or 16?

If you make a simple overcall with both:

♠ x x   ♡ A J x x x   ◊ A K J   ♣ K x x

♠ K Q 10 9 x x   ♡ x x   ◊ J 10 x x   ♣ x

how does partner know when to look for game and when not to, when to sacrifice and when to double the opponents? This problem has become soluble only in recent years, with the introduction of the preemptive single jump overcall.

WEAK JUMP OVERCALLS

Today, most American experts have switched from strong to preemptive jump overcalls. This has come about primarily because the hands suitable for strong jump overcalls occur so seldom. And even those rare hands can be handled as well or better by use of the takeout double. If your right-hand opponent opens one club and you hold:

♠ A K Q J x x   ♡ K 10 x   ◊ K J x   ♣ x

it is just as satisfactory to double first and then to jump in spades as it is to overcall two spades directly; in fact, it is preferable. In consequence, the strong jump overcall has become an "idle" bid, used perhaps once in two hundred deals. Could it not be given a different meaning, enabling it to do some real work?

What You Can Gain

So the idea developed of using the jump overcall as a weak bid, a mild preemptive device for hands without the freakish pattern which would justify a *double* jump, but with a good suit and little defensive strength. Clearly, it is ideal to jump to *three* spades over an opponent's one-club opening bid, if you hold:

♠ Q J 10 x x x x   ♡ x   ◊ x   ♣ A 10 9 x

You cut away almost all the enemy bidding room, and often responder will have no choice but to double you and accept a small plus score even when he is very strong. However, you seldom hold such freaks; more usually your hand will look like:

♠ Q J 10 x x x   ♡ x x   ◊ x x x   ♣ A x

Here a double-jump overcall is far too dangerous. The opponents are very likely to double, and at that level the penalty will give them an ample return for their high cards. Yet you would like to preempt, for you are weak defensively and have considerable offensive strength. A *one*-spade overcall will have some nuisance value, but it is a good deal more effective to be able to bid *two* spades. This mild preemptive action does not force the enemy to double you—it leaves them room for bidding; but it takes away two crucial rounds of auction, and they will not be able to bid accurately.

NORTH
♠ x x x
♡ Q x x x x
♢ K x
♣ K J x

WEST
♠ Q J 10 x x x
♡ x x
♢ x x x
♣ A x

EAST
♠ K x
♡ A 10 x
♢ Q J 10 x x x
♣ x x

SOUTH
♠ A x
♡ K J x
♢ A x
♣ Q 10 x x x

SOUTH	WEST	NORTH	EAST
1 ♣	1 ♠	2 ♣	2 ♢
2 NT	Pass	3 ♡	Pass
4 ♡	Pass	Pass	Pass

The one spade overcall embarrasses North, for he can no longer show his heart suit without overbidding. However, he gets another chance, and North-South reach their best contract. But:

SOUTH	WEST	NORTH	EAST
1 ♣	2 ♠	3 ♣	Pass
3 NT	Pass	Pass	Pass

The jump overcall is likely to do an effective job of jostling the opponents into an inferior contract. It will not always work; even here, North-South could land on their feet. But the jump overcall normally takes away so much bidding space that the opponents are guessing. And often they guess wrong.

One of the most common ways in which the weak jump overcall gains is by trapping the opponents into overbidding to a game contract. This hand is typical:

```
                      NORTH
                    ♠ K x x
                    ♡ K x x x
                    ◇ x x x
                    ♣ J 10 9

        WEST                        EAST
      ♠ x x x                     ♠ A 10 x x
      ♡ x                         ♡ x x
      ◇ A Q J 10 x x              ◇ K x
      ♣ x x x                     ♣ K Q x x x

                      SOUTH
                    ♠ Q J x
                    ♡ A Q J 10 x x
                    ◇ x x
                    ♣ A x
```

SOUTH	WEST	NORTH	EAST
1 ♡	2 ◇	2 ♡	3 ♣
3 ♡	Pass	Pass	Pass

If West makes a simple overcall (or passes), North-South will surely reach three hearts on some auction like that above—one heart, two hearts, three hearts, pass. But what if West jumps to *three* diamonds over one heart? If North bids three hearts, South will go to game; if North passes and South reopens with three hearts, *North* will bid game. And should both pass, West will make three diamonds.

In any variation, North-South will end up losing points even though they own the hand.

Negative Inferences from Failure to Jump

Clearly, the weak jump overcall can be an extremely useful device, destroying enemy communications without getting you up so high that the opponents have to double in self-defense. But perhaps its greatest value comes, paradoxically, in the hands in which it is *not* used. For whenever you make a *simple* overcall, your partner should wonder what there is about your hand which makes it unsuitable for a *jump* overcall.

Two possible answers suggest themselves: your hand might be too weak for a jump overcall—the suit not long and solid enough, the distribution too flat; or, your hand could be too strong—the game prospects too bright, the defensive strength too great for preemptive action. Suppose that your right-hand opponent opens one club and you hold:

♠ x x   ♡ K J x x x   ◇ K 10 x   ♣ Q x x

Obviously, you do not want to jump in hearts—it is far too dangerous. But should you bid *one* heart either? Test the hand by the standards set up earlier in this chapter. Your point-count does not indicate that you own the hand. You are not interested in a sacrifice, since your distribution is unexciting and you have scattered defensive values. You are not sure that you want a heart lead. A one-heart overcall will have little preemptive effect. So there is almost nothing to gain by bidding. And the overcall is perilous, for your suit is broken and you have no other suit to run to if doubled. Opponents who bid on hands like this one kept good players in champagne for years. Unhappily, the breed is becoming extinct; nowadays, experts have to write books.

The point is that just those features which make the

hand unsuitable for a *jump* overcall—the poor suit, the even pattern, the smattering of defense—make it unsuitable for a *simple* overcall as well. But add an ace to the hand:

♠ A x   ♡ K J x x x   ◊ K 10 x   ♣ Q x x

and it becomes a reasonable overcall. It is very nearly as dangerous to bid as before; the extra ace will decrease the size of any penalty, but will also decrease the amount the opponents could make, instead, by playing the hand themselves. However, there is a great deal more to be gained by bidding, since a real prospect now exists that the hand belongs to you, possibly for a game.

The conclusion that we are being driven towards, then, is this: *if your jump overcalls are preemptive, your simple overcalls are never made with weak hands.* Not that you must always have a powerhouse in order to overcall; but you should have a lively interest in getting to game. Otherwise, you would jump overcall if your suit were good enough or pass if it were not. And this is the corner-stone of modern defensive bidding.

MODERN DEFENSIVE BIDDING

Jump Overcall, Takeout Double, Simple Overcall

Classical defensive bidding relies on two basic tools— *the takeout double* for all hands rich in high cards, *the simple overcall* for light distributional hands. Modern defensive bidding has three. *The jump overcall* caters to all the weak hands with which you wish to enter the auction in order to find a sacrifice, direct an opening lead, or disrupt enemy communications; and it does a better job of it than would a simple overcall. For strong hands, which may make game opposite a partner who could not bid independently, you have *the takeout double* and *the simple overcall.*

The distinction between the double and the overcall is not your point-count but your distributional pattern. You do not double because you are too strong to overcall. You double when you believe that the hand will play best in partner's longest unbid suit; you can support them all. You overcall when there is an unbid suit which you cannot support, or when you believe that the hand will play best in your own long suit.

Examples

Let us return to our earlier example hands, and see how they would be handled in modern style.

(a) ♠ K Q 10 9 x x   ♡ x x   ◊ J 10 x x   ♣ x

Over an opposing one-club opening, this is an ideal *jump to two spades*. Thereby, you encourage partner to take a sacrifice, suggest a spade opening lead, and rob the opponents of two rounds of bidding.

(b) ♠ x x   ♡ A J x x x   ◊ A K J   ♣ K x x

Overcall one heart after a one-club opening. You cannot support spades, and have a distinct preference for play in hearts. The simple overcall tells partner that you are interested in game if he has a fair hand. And it keeps you at a low level if he has a bust. As we have seen, it is more dangerous to go to the two-level with this hand than with the first one, since *here* the opponents cannot make much on their own, and any set will be a true loss.

(c) ♠ J x x   ♡ A Q x x   ◊ K J x x   ♣ x

Double an opening bid of one club for takeout. Although your point-count is not exciting, your excellent support for all unbid suits suggests game possibilities, and, at the same time, provides a considerable measure of safety. Your double assures partner of support for his best suit, and urges him to compete at as high a level as his hand warrants. Note that you yourself have no preference for a trump suit; the takeout double has its inherent meaning—you want to play in partner's suit.

In fact, modern defensive bidding is all very natural. Whenever you have a strong suit, you bid it—at a minimum level if your hand, as well as your suit, is strong; with a jump if your hand is weak. You double when you do not know what the trump suit should be. As a result, your partner will always be in a position to make an informed decision instead of a guess, even when the opponents crowd the auction with a preemptive jump over your defensive bid.

2

THE TAKEOUT DOUBLE

♠ ♡ ◇ ♣

REQUIREMENTS FOR DOUBLE

When is a double for takeout instead of for penalties?

First, partner must have done nothing but pass. If he has bid, you can be in possession of enough information to warrant a penalty double; but if he hasn't, you are unlikely to believe that you can set a low contract all by yourself.

Second, it must *be* a fairly low contract that you are doubling. When you double a contract of four spades or higher, you are doubling primarily for penalties.

Third, it must be your first opportunity to double the suit that is bid. On an auction like:

OPENER	YOU	RESPONDER	PARTNER
1 ♡	Pass	1 NT	Pass
2 ♡	*Double*		

your double is for penalties. Had you wanted to hear from partner, you would have doubled *one* heart; instead, you set a trap, and now have sprung it. (An exception to this third rule, which we will explore later, is the delayed double of a suit which has been raised.)

All three of these conditions must be met in order for your double to be for takeout. In effect, then, a takeout double is almost always made right over the opening bid, or else over the first response when partner has passed.

Distributional Requirements

There are two sets of requirements for a takeout double. The first, and more important, concerns distribution: *you must have at least three-card support for all unbid suits.* If you double an opening bid of one heart, you do not have a void, singleton, or even a doubleton in spades, diamonds or clubs. (And you are very likely to have *four* spades, not three, since your takeout double begs partner to respond in the unbid major suit; as we will see, he should strain to do so.)

Do not fear that this strict distributional requirement will limit the usefulness of the takeout double by making it a rare bid. It will be your most frequent defensive action, for, since the opening bid is in your opponent's longest suit, your most common pattern is to be short in opener's suit and long in the other three. And the relatively low point-count requirements will allow you to double with a majority of the hands that have this likely distribution.

Obviously, however, you cannot double with them all. If your opponent opens with one diamond and you hold:

♠ Q x x x   ♡ J x x x   ◇ x   ♣ Q 10 x x

you might well have a wistful inclination to double, since your distribution is ideal. But you must resist the temptation and pass—if you were to double with hands this weak, partner could never tell when to go to game, or when to double the enemy. A minimum point-count requirement is necessary.

Point Count Requirements

In counting points for a takeout double, value your hand in *support* of partner's response. That is, add to your high-card points extra points for shortness. Your only short suit will be the enemy's.

If you are void, in opponent's suit add 5 points to your high-card count.

If you have a singleton in opponent's suit, add 3 points.

With a doubleton in opponent's suit, add 1 point.

But *do not* count minor honors—queens or jacks—in the enemy suit.

And pay careful attention to your length in any unbid *major* suit, the most likely response to your double. If the opening bid is one spade or one heart, subtract one point when you have only three-card support for the other major.

If the opening is one club or one diamond, subtract a point if you do not have at least one four-card major suit.

How many points do you need in order to double? Eleven points are sufficient if partner can respond at the *one* level; that is, if you are doubling a bid of one heart or lower.

But when your double forces partner to bid at the *two* level (when you double one spade or higher), you should have at least 2 points more—13 points is the minimum. The requirement goes up 2 points for each level of bidding. To double two spades:

OPENER	PARTNER	RESPONDER	YOU
1 ♠	Pass	2 ♠	Double

and force a response at the three-level, you should have 15 points.

And had responder bid *three* spades, you would need 17 points to double.

When you double a response of one-notrump:

OPENER	PARTNER	RESPONDER	YOU
1 ♡	Pass	1 NT	Double

you are making a takeout double of opener's suit, just as if you had doubled directly over the opening bid. The requirements are identical, except that since partner must bid at the two-level regardless of the suit opened, the 13-point minimum applies.

Vulnerability conditions can modify all these point-count requirements somewhat. If you are vulnerable and the opponents are not, competition is more dangerous. The enemy will be itching to double your partner's response for penalties, and if he is set 800 points it will not soothe him to whip out a copy of this book and prove that you had enough for a takeout double. It is better to be on the safe side, and have an extra point or two. However, when the opponents are vulnerable and you are not, competition is safe and often rewarding. Therefore, you can shade down all minimum requirements by 1 point. On equal vulnerability, the rules apply as stated.

Quiz

Do you double with these example hands?

(a) No one vulnerable, right-hand opponent opens one club. You hold:

♠ A J x x   ♡ K x x   ◊ Q x x x   ♣ x x

(b) Both vulnerable, right-hand opponent opens one spade. You hold:

♠ J x   ♡ Q J x   ◊ A Q J x   ♣ J x x x

(c) You are not vulnerable against vulnerable opponents. One heart is opened to your left, partner passes, right-hand opponent bids two hearts. You hold:

♠ J 10 x x   ♡ Void   ◊ A x x x   ♣ Q 10 x x x

(d) You are vulnerable against non-vulnerable opponents. One diamond is opened to your right. You hold:

♠ A K x x   ♡ x x   ◇ K x   ♣ A 10 x x x

(a) *Double.* You have 11 points—10 in high cards plus 1 for the doubleton club—and have a four-card major suit, so there is no deduction. Vulnerable against non-vulnerable opponents, you should pass. Non-vulnerable against vulnerable, you might double without the spade jack.

(b) *Pass.* This hand has a value of only 11 points—11 in high cards (you do not count the spade jack) plus 1 point for the doubleton, but minus 1 point for holding only three-card support for hearts, the likely response. Since a double would force partner to bid at the two-level, 13 points is the minimum. If the opening bid were one diamond and your spade and diamond holdings were reversed, you should double. Partner could then respond at the one-level, and your point-count would be sufficient.

(c) *Double.* You have 12 points—7 in high cards and 5 for the void. Normally, 13 points would be required to double two hearts, but on this vulnerability you can be 1 point light. You are quite likely to find a cheap sacrifice against a vulnerable game contract.

(d) *Do not double.* You have more than enough points, but you may not double with a doubleton in an unbid suit. As we will see later, this hand qualifies for an overcall.

RESPONDING TO A TAKEOUT DOUBLE

The takeout double is a forcing call. If there is no intervening bid, you may not pass partner's double no matter how weak you are; the less you have, the more the opponents will score at their doubled contract. Remember that doubler's hand is probably of the wrong pattern for defense; the shorter he is in the enemy suit, the more likely he is to double.

Penalty Pass

Of course, if partner doubles a one-heart opening bid and you hold:

♠ x   ♡ K Q J 10 x x   ◇ K x x   ♣ x x x

you should pass the double for penalties. But the *penalty pass* requires a hand just about as extreme as this example. You must have the solid holding which will enable you to draw trumps. With:

♠ J x x   ♡ Q 10 8 x x   ◇ x x x   ♣ x x

do not even consider passing a double of one heart; you must respond one spade, your cheapest three-card suit. You should pass a takeout double for penalties perhaps once a year, and that often only if you play bridge a great deal too frequently.

Negative or Positive Response

Since you are virtually compelled to respond to a take-out double, your forced response promises no values whatever. Let me introduce you to the "little monster":

♠ x x x x   ♡ x x x   ◇ x x x   ♣ x x x

When you respond one spade to partner's takeout double, you may well have the hand above. And this is the key to all auctions which follow a takeout double. Doubler must not bid again without substantial extra values, for fear that partner holds the "little monster." Therefore, the doubler's partner must not bid as if he held the "little monster" when he has real strength of his own, for fear of missing game.

The minimum forced response to a takeout double:

OPENER	PARTNER	RESPONDER	YOU
1 ♣	Double	Pass	1 ◇ , 1 ♡ or 1 ♠

is a denial. It is a *negative* response, like the two-notrump reply to a forcing two-bid. You may have no strength at all; you may have as many as 7 or 8 points (in which case you intend to bid again voluntarily if you get the chance). But you may not have more. With 9 points, your hand is so much better than the "little monster" that you must make a *positive*, not a negative, response—a jump bid.

Counting Points as Responder

When responding to a takeout double, count your points as if you were supporting partner, since he has guaranteed length in all unbid suits.

Add to your high card count 1 point for every card over four in any unbid suit.

And add 1 point for each doubleton, 3 points for each singleton, 5 points for a void.

But discount values in the opponents' suit. Do not value the queen or jack at all.

And count the king as only 2 points unless it is behind the bidder.

Add 1 point fewer for shortness in the enemy suit (void–4; singleton–2; doubleton–0) since partner is short also, and the distribution is worth less, being duplicated.

Quiz

What is the point value of your hand, and what is your response in the following examples? In each case, the auction has gone:

OPENER	PARTNER	RESPONDER	YOU
1 ◇	Double	Pass	?

(a) ♠ Q x x x ♡ K Q x x ◇ Q x ♣ x x x

(b) ♠ K x ♡ J x x x x ◇ x x ♣ A x x x

(c) ♠ 10 x x x ♡ x x x ◇ x ♣ Q J x x x

(d) ♠ x ♡ Q J x x ◇ J x x ♣ K 10 x x x

(e) ♠ x x ♡ x x ◇ 10 x x x x ♣ J x x x

(a) ♠ Q x x x ♡ K Q x x ◇ Q x ♣ x x x

Bid one spade. You have 7 points (counting nothing for either the queen or the doubleton in the opponent's suit), close to a maximum for the negative response. Since you plan to bid again if possible, you start with the higher-ranking suit. The auction might well go:

OPENER	PARTNER	RESPONDER	YOU
1 ◇	Double	Pass	1 ♠
2 ♣	Pass	2 ◇	2 ♡

Now partner can choose between the two major suits without increasing the level of bidding. Note that it is up to *you* to fight for the part-score. Partner cannot compete further, even with a sound, 16-point double, for fear that you hold the "little monster."

(b) ♠ K x ♡ J x x x x ◇ x x ♣ A x x x

Jump to two hearts. Your hand is worth 10 points—8 points in high cards, plus one point each for the fifth heart and the doubleton spade (nothing for the doubleton diamond). You must make a positive response.

(c) ♠ 10 x x x ♡ x x x ◇ x ♣ Q J x x x

Bid one spade. Value this hand at 6 points—3 points in high cards, 1 point for the fifth club, 2 points for the singleton in the enemy suit. You respond in spades, not in clubs, because it is a major suit. If you have a game, or if you can buy the contract for a part-score, it is most likely to be in the high-ranking suit. It usually pays to suppress even a *six*-card minor suit in order to respond to a double in a four-card major.

(d) ♠ x ♡ Q J x x ◇ J x x ♣ K 10 x x x

Jump to two hearts. This hand is quite a lot stronger than it looks, for the distributional "fit" is excellent—partner is short in diamonds, you are short in spades. You have 10 points—6 points in high cards (discounting the diamond jack), 1 point for the fifth club, 3 points for the singleton spade.

Note that you should jump in the major suit, where game is likely, not in the minor, Do not be afraid of four-card suits in response to a double; partner has at least three hearts and probably has four. In effect, you are supporting him, and four-card *support* is nothing to be ashamed of.

(e) ♠ x x ♡ x x ◇ 10 x x x x ♣ J x x x

Bid two clubs. It is inconceivable either to pass the double or to respond one notrump, holding so little strength and such weak diamonds. It is unpleasant to go to the two-level with only 3 points, but you have no option. Partner cannot expect any greater strength for this negative response, and two clubs should not be a horrible contract, since partner must have at least three-card support.

Moreover, if you *are* doubled in two clubs and penalized heavily, you can give yourself the pleasure of blaming the disaster on your partner. It's his fault, not yours.

Cue Bid Response

You will have noticed that the jump response to a take-out double does not promise a very strong hand. This merely positive response is not forcing to game, like a jump response to an opening bid. Indeed, it is not even forcing for one round. Doubler is invited to move toward game if he has extra strength, but half the time he will pass the jump.

Therefore, bids stronger than the jump responses are needed. It is all very well to extend a mild invitation when you have 9, 10 or 11 points; but you will miss games unless you are more forceful when you have a greater count.

All stronger sequences are initiated by the cue-bid of the opponents' suit:

OPENER	PARTNER	RESPONDER	YOU
1 ♡	Double	Pass	2 ♡

This cue-bid has nothing whatever to do with your holding in the enemy suit; you do not promise first-round, or second-round, or even third-round control. The cue-bid says, "Partner, we're almost certainly on our way to a game contract somewhere. Let's explore." For the auction above, you might hold:

♠ K Q x x   ♡ x x x   ◇ A Q 10 x x   ♣ x

With a hand worth 15 points, you are too strong for a jump to two spades, or to three diamonds, for partner might pass. You want to be in game, but where? The way to find out is to force with the cue-bid. If doubler answers two spades, you will jump to four spades. If he answers three clubs, you can now bid three diamonds without fear of being passed there, for you have described a hand too strong for an immediate jump.

However, even this cue-bid is not unconditionally forcing to *game*. A 12– or 13-point hand does not guarantee a sound play for game opposite a bare minimum double of 11 or 12 points. Suppose you hold:

♠ K Q J x   ♡ A J x x   ◇ x x   ♣ x x x

Left-hand opponent opens one club, partner doubles, and responder passes. With 12 points you are too strong for a jump response, so you must cue-bid two clubs. But if partner answers your cue-bid with two hearts or two spades, you will raise not to game but to *three*. And doubler may now pass if he holds a bare minimum. Every *new suit* bid by the cue-bidder is forcing, but any *raise* is merely a strong invitation. Let us examine a more complex auction:

	PARTNER		YOU
	♠ 10 x x x		♠ K Q J x
	♡ K Q x		♡ A J x x
	◇ Q J 10 x x		◇ x x
	♣ x		♣ x x x

OPENER	PARTNER	RESPONDER	YOU
1 ♣	Double	Pass	2 ♣
Pass	2 ◇	Pass	2 ♡
Pass	2 ♠	Pass	3 ♠
Pass	Pass	Pass	

Your cue-bid is, of course, forcing, and partner answers by bidding his best suit. Partner cannot pass your two-heart bid either, for it is a new suit, and he bids again even with his scratchy minimum double. But your third bid is a raise—an invitation, not a command. So partner passes gratefully.

Free Response

So far, we have assumed that opening bidder's partner will pass after your partner's double. If, instead, he re-doubles, bids a new suit, or raises preemptively, your response to the double may be affected. For one thing, you are no longer compelled to bid; partner will get a second chance to speak anyway. For another, responder's action may have used up too much bidding space to permit your natural answer to be made.

AT THE ONE LEVEL

The fact that you are no longer forced to bid does not mean that you *must* pass, or that you need great strength for any action. Of course, if you hold the "little monster" and the auction goes:

OPENER	PARTNER	RESPONDER	YOU
1 ♣	Double	1 ◇ or	?
		1 ♡ or	
		Redouble	

you will seize the opportunity to pass with a (silent) sigh of relief. However, if you have 6 points or so, or even if you hold fewer points but have a long suit, make an effort to bid. On the auction above, either of these hands:

♠ K J x x   ♡ x x   ◇ Q x x x   ♣ x x x
♠ Q J 10 x x   ♡ x x   ◇ x x x x   ♣ x x

is a proper "free" response of one spade. When you can act at the one-level, bid if you have any feature that is attractive; pass only if you would have hated to respond were you forced to.

JUMP RESPONSES

It follows, therefore, that you must still jump with 9– to 11-point hands; a "free" bid does not do justice to such strength. If you hold:

♠ A 10 x x x   ♡ x x   ◇ K 10 x x   ♣ x x

you should bid:

OPENER	PARTNER	RESPONDER	YOU
1 ♣	Double	1 ♡	2 ♠

You would bid *one* spade without the diamond king.

AT HIGHER LEVELS

A higher bid by responder over partner's double will, like any action which robs you of bidding room, cause trouble. On this auction:

OPENER	PARTNER	RESPONDER	YOU
1 ♣	Double	2 ♣	2 ♠

it is not clear whether you had intended to *jump* to two spades over one club doubled, or whether you would have bid only a cheerful one spade. On the auction above, you should bid two spades with both of these hands:

(a) ♠ K J 10 x x x   ♡ x x   ◇ x x x   ♣ x x
(b) ♠ K 10 x x   ♡ x x   ◇ K Q x x   ♣ x x x

Yet with hand (a)—7 points—you would have bid only one spade except for the intervening raise; with hand (b)—9 points—you would have jumped to two spades anyway. (Obviously, you can no longer afford to jump with hand (b). *Three* spades could be a dangerously high contract facing a minimum double, and partner might bid a losing game when he has 14 or 15 points.) Necessarily, different point ranges must be assigned to responses in order to handle high competitive bids.

Fortunately, a simple rule takes care of all auctions: you need 2 points extra for each additional level to which you are forced to bid. For example, a free response at the one-level has a range of 5 to 8 points; so, to make the same non-jump response at the *two*-level, you need 7 to 10 points. Similarly, a jump response at the two-level promises 9 to 11 points; if an intervening raise forces you to jump to the *three*-level, you require 11 to 13 points. And violent preemptive action by the enemy may force you to add *4* points to the requirements.

EXAMPLES

OPENER	PARTNER	RESPONDER	YOU
1 ♡	Double	3 ♡	?

The non-jump free bid of three spades would here require 9 points instead of 5 points. And the *jump* response, to *four* spades, requires 13 points not 9. On the auction above, with:

♠ K J x x　♡ x x　♢ x x x　♣ Q J x x

you must *pass*. Had the intervening raise been to only two hearts, you would have mustered up a free response of two spades. But 7 points is not enough for a bid at the three level. With:

♠ K J x x　♡ x x　♢ x x x　♣ K Q J x

bid three spades. Without the interference, you would

have jumped in spades. Now 11 points is not enough for a jump, but you can bid freely at the three-level.

On the same auction, with:

♠ K J x x   ♡ x x   ◇ K x x   ♣ K Q J x

bid four spades. But for the interference, you would have cue-bid and then given partner a chance to pass under game. If the intervening raise were only to *two* hearts, you would have jumped to *three* spades, urging, but not forcing, partner to go on. Here, however, the enemy has robbed you of these delicate sequences. Thirteen points is the minimum strength for this jump to game—9 points for a jump response p!us 4 points for the two additional levels required.

Notrump Responses

Only rarely should you respond in notrump to partner's takeout double. Just those distributional features which make a hand attractive for a takeout double make it unattractive as the dummy in a notrump contract. Doubler wants to hear a suit, and you should almost always oblige him.

Never answer one notrump to a double when you have a weak hand with no suit to bid. If partner doubles a one-spade opening bid and you must respond with:

♠ Q 10 x x   ♡ x x x   ◇ x x x   ♣ x x x

bid two clubs, not one notrump. Notrump contracts are the easiest ones for the enemy to double for penalties—to double you, all they need is points, not a strong holding in any particular suit. And when you are this weak, they have points to spare.

In contrast, you are most unlikely to be hurt if you respond in a suit. Opener cannot double for penalties, and any bid he makes will take your neck off the chopping-block. So do not be afraid to bid even an honorless three-card suit; be afraid to bid notrump.

The one-notrump response to partner's takeout double is a strong bid—a positive response. It can be made with an evenly distributed hand of 9 points or more which contains two stoppers in the enemy suit. For example, when partner doubles a one-diamond opening bid, answer one notrump with:

♠ Q x x   ♡ x x x   ◊ K J 10 x   ♣ Q J x

This response has the range of 9 to 11 points.

With 12 to 14 points, jump to two notrump, strongly urging partner to go on if he is not ashamed of his high-card content.

With more strength still, cue-bid the opponent's suit.

A different hand pattern which calls for a notrump response consists of a long unbid minor suit plus a stopper in the enemy suit. Again, notrump is a constructive response. You promise at least 9 points, counting extra points for length, but not, of course, for shortness. So if partner doubles a one-heart opening bid and you hold:

♠ x x   ♡ K x x   ◊ x x x   ♣ Q 10 x x x

sign off with the negative two-club response. But if you hold:

♠ x x   ♡ K x x   ◊ x x x   ♣ K Q 10 x x

encourage with a response of one notrump. And holding:

♠ x x   ♡ K x x   ◊ Q x   ♣ A Q 10 x x x

jump to two notrump.

Note that you do not require stoppers in side suits for these notrump responses. Partner's double promises length in all unbid suits; your concern is to stop opener's suit and provide enough strength for safety. Observe also that no example is given of a notrump response when holding four cards in an unbid *major* suit. Preference should always be given to the major suit response; notrump can be bid secondarily if doubler moves toward game.

DOUBLER'S REBID

Since partner's response to your takeout double is so explicit, you have an easy task finding the proper action at your second turn. If game is not in view, you pass; if game is possible but not certain, you bid again; if game is sure, you jump right to it or force.

Twenty-five points in the combined hands is the magic number for a major-suit game. (The usual figure of 26 allows for a little wasted strength. However, after an opponent's opening it is possible to know which values are "working." The 25 points do not include useless honors in the enemy suit or duplicated distribution.) When you have doubled and partner has responded, ask yourself whether your points added to partner's can total 25.

Over Minimum Reply

If partner has made a minimum forced reply, a negative response, his top limit is 8 points. Thus, there is no chance for game when you have 16 points or fewer. *Do not bid again.* There is very little to gain by bidding and the loss may be great, for partner may hold the "little monster." Suppose that you have doubled a one-heart opening bid with:

♠ A Q x x   ♡ x x   ◊ K x x   ♣ A J x x

Left-hand opponent passes and partner responds one spade. If opener passes, you must pass also—game is impossible, since partner has fewer than 9 points and you have only 15. Even if opener bids two hearts over partner's one-spade response, do not raise spades. True, the hand may belong to your side for a spade partial, but it is *partner* who must compete, not you. If he holds 5 or 6 points, the sort of hand with which he could have bid one spade freely, he will bid again. Do not feel that you must show your spade support by raising; you have shown it by doubling. Partner knows that you have at least three spades and most likely four. Therefore, if he holds:

♠ K x x x ♡ x x x ◇ x x ♣ Q x x x

the auction might well go:

OPENER	YOU	RESPONDER	PARTNER
1 ♡	Double	Pass	1 ♠
2 ♡	Pass	Pass	2 ♠

Observe that partner can rebid a four-card suit; when you double one heart, he is actually supporting *your* spade suit. His second bid shows a little high-card strength, not extra spade length. And it enables you to compete as high as three spades, if necessary, when you have four cards in spades and about 15 points. However, neither of you is going to bid game—this is impossible when partner could not jump at his first turn and you could not bid at your second.

When your double is made with a hand worth 17 points or more, a minimum response does not preclude game. Therefore, you must bid again. If partner has responded in a major suit for which you have four-card support, you will raise—a single raise with 17 to 19 points, a jump raise with 20 to 22 points. (If you have four-card support for a *minor* suit, you may raise, but should prefer instead to bid a strong major suit or notrump whenever possible.) On this auction:

OPENER	YOU	RESPONDER	PARTNER
1 ◇	Double	Pass	1 ♠
Pass	?		

Bid two spades if your hand is:

♠ K Q x x ♡ A 10 x ◇ x ♣ K Q 10 x x

You have 17 points (adding 3 for the singleton diamond) so game is possible. However, you will pass at your next turn if partner now raises to three spades; as he will with

6 or 7 points. You have the minimum for your bid, and partner would jump all the way to game if he held 8 points, his maximum.

If on the same auction your hand is:

♠ K Q x x   ♡ A K x   ◇ x   ♣ A Q 10 x x

Jump to *three* spades. You will go down when partner has the "little monster," but if he has any values at all—the ace of spades, the king of clubs, a side singleton, etc.—he will bid and make game.

Any raise promises four-card support. With 17 points or more, but with only three cards in partner's suit, try for game by bidding a suit of your own (or notrump). If you have doubled a one-club opening, holding:

♠ A Q x   ♡ K Q 10 x x   ◇ A Q x   ♣ x x

you should rebid two hearts over a one-spade response, or one heart over a one-diamond response. This does not "deny" partner's suit, for you would have overcalled instead of doubling if you lacked three-card support for an unbid suit. Partner can safely rebid a five-card or longer suit; he can jump in such a suit to invite game with 6 or 7 points; he can even jump all the way to game in his own suit with an 8-point hand (he can add to 25 points, since you promise 17 by rebidding; he can add to eight trumps if he has five, since you guarantee three by doubling).

If you have a maximum double—20 to 22 points—but lack four-card support for partner, you may *jump* in your own suit. This strongly urges, but does not force, partner to bid game somewhere. Alternatively, you may use the delayed cue-bid—the bid of the enemy suit over partner's response:

OPENER	YOU	RESPONDER	PARTNER
1 ◇	Double	Pass	1 ♠
Pass	2 ◇		

This is forcing for one round, and shows an unusually

powerful double. However, it tends to deny four cards in partner's suit (you would raise) or a long suit of your own (you would jump in it). For the auction above, you might hold:

♠ A Q x　♡ A K J x　◇ x x　♣ A K 10 x

Over Positive Reply

When partner's response to your double has been positive—a jump—his top limit is 11 points. Thus, you will pass all hands worth 13 points or fewer. If you hold a 14— or 15-point double, the combined count of 25 points which you need for game is possible but not sure. Therefore, you raise partner's suit (if you have four-card support) asking him to go on with a maximum, to pass with a minimum. And when your double is worth 16 points or more, you can jump right to game if you are sure of the trump suit. Note that any raise still promises four-card support, even though partner has made a jump response. If you have the strength to move toward game, but have only three cards in partner's suit, bid a new suit of your own.

Over a positive response, doubler's change of suit is forcing. After jumping, partner can pass at his next turn only when doubler *raises*. When doubler bids a new suit, his hand is unlimited in strength—he may even have slam ambitions.

Quiz

You have doubled a one-diamond opening bid, and partner has jumped to two hearts in reply. What is your rebid with these hands?

(a) ♠ A J x x　♡ K Q x x　◇ x x　♣ J 10 x

(b) ♠ K Q x　♡ K 10 x x　◇ x　♣ K 10 x x x

(c) ♠ A Q x x x　♡ K Q x　◇ x　♣ K 10 x x

(d) ♠ A K x x x　♡ K Q x x　◇ x　♣ Q x x

(a) *Pass*. With 12 points opposite a maximum of 11 points, game is out of the question.

(b) *Three hearts*. Fourteen points may be enough for game if partner has a maximum jump.

(c) *Two spades*. You have more than enough strength for game, but you may not raise with only three trumps.

(d) *Four hearts*. Your 17 points ensure a fine play for game opposite a jump. There is no need to bid spades; a good trump suit has already been found and there is no bonus for discovering another.

In all other auctions, just as in the common ones treated in detail in this section, doubler's rebid is determined by adding his points to partner's and observing the chance of totalling to 25. For instance, suppose the bidding goes:

OPENER	YOU	RESPONDER	PARTNER
1 ♡	Double	Pass	2 ♡
Pass	2 ♠	Pass	3 ♠

Partner has 12 or 13 points—too much for a jump, not enough to bid game over two spades. So go to game unless you have 11 points or a bare, scrawny 12 points for your double.

Another example:

OPENER	YOU	RESPONDER	PARTNER
1 ♡	Double	2 ♡	2 ♠

Partner has 7 to 10 points, 2 points more than the range for a free response at the one-level. So pass with 14 points or fewer; raise to three spades with four trumps and 15 to 17 points, to four spades with 18 points or more. (Bid a new suit with 15 points or more, when holding only three-card support.)

TWO-SUIT DOUBLES

Occasionally, you will make a takeout double after the opponents have bid *two* suits:

OPENER	PARTNER	RESPONDER	YOU
1 ◇	Pass	1 ♠	Double

Requirements

The requirements for this double are nominally unchanged: support for each unbid suit; 11 points if partner can bid at the one-level; 13 points if he must bid at the two-level (as in the example auction), and 2 points more for each additional level. Now, of course, doubler can count for shortness in *two* enemy suits. And this makes an enormous difference, for it allows the double to be made with a rather weak two-suited freak. For the example auction above, you might well hold:

♠ x   ♡ K 10 x x x   ◇ x   ♣ K Q x x x x

With 8 points in high cards and 3 points extra for each singleton, you add to 14 points—more than enough to double. Actually, the two-suit double normally contains at least nine or ten cards in the unbid suits; occasionally you may have four of each. Rarely, though, should you have only three-card support for an unbid suit. With flat distribution, it cannot pay for you to contest the auction against two bidding oponents (with a passing partner) unless you have overwhelming high-card strength—more power than the two of them combined. And that won't be often.

So, although the double after the opponents have bid two suits has the same requirements as a normal double, the hand is likely to look quite different. This double is, in effect, an overcall in *both* unbid suits.

Responses

In responding to a two-suit double, your prime duty is to take a choice between partner's two suits. This means that you will often have to bid a three-card suit. Consider the auction:

OPENER	YOU	RESPONDER	PARTNER
1 ♣	Pass	1 ♡	Double
Pass	?		

If your hand is:

♠ x x x   ♡ Q x x   ◊ J x   ♣ K 10 x x x

you must bid one spade. Partner should not get enthusiastic even if, as is likely, he holds five spades. He must remember that he has put a gun to your back and forced you to respond. You might well have less.

If you have much more, it is up to *you* to get enthusiastic. On the auction above, this is a mountain of a hand:

♠ A Q x x   ♡ x x x x   ◊ Q x   ♣ x x x

All your high cards are working, and your doubleton faces partner's length. Holding 9 points, you must jump to *two* spades.

But with:

♠ K x x x   ♡ K J x x   ◊ x x x   ♣ Q x

bid only *one* spade. Remember to devalue honors in the enemy suits, and not to count for shortness where partner is short also.

Whenever possible, avoid responding in notrump to a two-suit double. Almost surely, the notrump response is the last thing partner wants to hear. If you have any tolerance for one of the unbid suits, bid it. You are supporting partner, not bidding a suit of your own.

Free Responses

If opener bids over partner's double:

OPENER	YOU	RESPONDER	PARTNER
1 ◊	Pass	1 ♡	Double
2 ♡	?		

you are no longer forced to bid. But almost any 5– or 6-point hand is worth a free bid when you have four cards in one of partner's suits. If, on the auction above, you hold:

♠ Q x x x   ♡ 10 x x x   ◇ A x x   ♣ x x

bid two spades. If partner has a really freakish hand, you will have a spectacularly successful sacrifice (or even a make) at four spades. Visualize partner's hand as a black two-suiter, perhaps:

♠ K 10 x x x   ♡ x   ◇ x x   ♣ A Q x x x

and you will see why you must get into the auction.

TAKEOUT DOUBLES BY A PASSED HAND

In auctions in which you have had the opportunity to open the bidding but have passed, you can be much more frisky with your takeout doubles. If you pass originally, left-hand opponent and partner pass also, and fourth hand opens one heart, all these hands are perfectly proper takeout doubles (except in unfavorable vulnerability):

♠ Q x x x   ♡ x   ◇ K J x x   ♣ J 10 x x
♠ J x x x x   ♡ None   ◇ A x x x   ♣ J x x x
♠ K Q x x   ♡ x x   ◇ A 10 x x   ♣ x x x

Observe that the "friskiness" applies only to high-card content, not to pattern. In fact, the distributional requirements are even more rigid, for you cannot have a wealth of high cards to compensate.

A takeout double of a major suit made by a passed hand guarantees at least four cards in the other major.

And a two-suit double by a passed hand almost always contains at least five cards in each unbid suit.

Respond to passed-hand doubles exactly as you would to a normal double, bearing in mind that you are looking to find a sacrifice, not a game. And be even more reluctant than usual to double the opponents for penalties after partner's takeout double. A passed-hand double does not promise defensive values; it is normally based on little more than good distribution and iron nerves.

3

THE OVERCALL

♠   ♡   ◇   ♣

WHEN TO OVERCALL

When should you overcall—enter the auction over an opponent's opening by bidding a suit of your own?

First, you must have a hand strong enough to give you hope of game even if partner could not bid independently.

Second, you must have a reason not to make a takeout double instead; such as an unbid suit for which you have no support, a long strong trump suit of your own, or two suits which you wish to bid yourself.

The overcall has nearly the identical range of strength of the opening one-bid in a suit. It is helpful to keep this similarity in mind. But there are differences too; as we have seen, the overcall is much more dangerous than is an opening bid. Many hands in the minimum opening bid range do not qualify as overcalls. When you weigh their *extent of risk* against their *chance for gain,* the balance tips against them.

Trump Value of Suits

"Extent of risk" is determined almost entirely by the quality of your suit. Ask yourself, "How many *more* tricks will my suit take if it is trump than it will take on defense?" It is this excess of offensive over defensive tricks which is the measure of a trump suit's real safety. A holding like:

♡ Q J 10 9 x x

will take 4 tricks if it is trump, but will not win any tricks if it is not. Contrast this with a holding like:

♡ A K Q J

Here again you have 4 offensive tricks, but now you have the likelihood of at least 2 defensive tricks as well. Thus, this holding has a real value of only 2 additional tricks *as a trump suit,* where the first example had a true value of 4 additional tricks, *as a trump suit.*

In estimating this "trump-value" of your suit, count:

(1) Every card over four as a trump-value.

(2) A card which is in sequence with two higher honors (or just barely out of sequence) as a trump-value.

Do *not* count aces and kings (or A-Q or K-Q combinations) which will win defensive tricks.

EXAMPLES

Assume that your hand qualifies in other respects as an overcall, and note the trump-value of these suits in which you might be tempted to overcall:

$$
\begin{array}{ll}
\text{A K Q 6 3} & = 2 \\
\text{K Q 10 6} & = 1 \\
\text{Q 10 6 4 3} & = 1 \\
\text{A J 8 6 5 4} & = 2 \\
\text{A Q J 10 6} & = 3 \\
\text{K Q J 10 7 3} & = 4
\end{array}
$$

As a rough guide, this figure for the trump-value of your suit coincides with the *level* at which it begins to be a little risky to bid such a suit. That is, you are safe in bidding a suit worth 3 trump-values at the two-level (you may go down, but the enemy would score more points playing with their own suit as trump); you incur a slight risk at the three-level, and you take a big chance at the four-level. A suit worth 1 trump-value makes an overcall somewhat risky at the one-level, dangerous at the two-level, almost inconceivable any higher.

Quick Tricks

However, on certain hands, the odds may favor making a dangerous overcall. It is your "chance for gain"—your prospects of making game—which determines how much risk it will pay you to assume. Just as suit quality measures safety, so the high-card structure of your whole hand measures the likelihood of game facing a partner who cannot bid independently. Here, the most reliable guide is the Quick Trick table:

$$
\begin{array}{rcl}
A\,K &=& 2 \\
A\,Q &=& 1\tfrac{1}{2} \\
A\ \ &=& 1 \\
K\,Q &=& 1 \\
K\ \ &=& \tfrac{1}{2}
\end{array}
$$

With fewer than $1\tfrac{1}{2}$ Quick Tricks, you have no chance for game (unless partner acts), so do not overcall.

With $1\tfrac{1}{2}$ to 2 Quick Tricks, overcall only if completely safe, for there is little chance for game.

However, with $2\tfrac{1}{2}$ or 3 Quick Tricks, be willing to assume a little risk since your game prospects are less remote.

And with $3\tfrac{1}{2}$ or 4 Quick Tricks make even dangerous overcalls, for your hand has really bright game prospects.

EXAMPLES

Let us see how this works in a few example hands.

♠ J x x   ♡ K Q x x x   ◊ A Q x   ♣ x x

Your right-hand opponent opens the bidding with one diamond; should you overcall one heart? You meet the preliminary test for an overcall—you would have opened the bidding as dealer. You may not double (because you lack support for clubs). What about risk versus gain? Your suit is worth only 1 trump-value, so a one-level overcall assumes some risk; but you have 2½ Quick Tricks, so it will pay in the long run to take the chance. Therefore, overcall.

However, suppose that the opening bid is one spade. Now your suit makes the overcall—at the *two*-level—highly dangerous. Your high-card structure does not warrant assuming this much risk. Therefore, you should pass.

Contrast this with a hand like:

♠ A x x   ♡ A Q x x x   ◊ A Q x   ♣ x x

Here, your high-card structure of 4 Quick Tricks makes game prospects so rosy that you should risk an overcall of two hearts after a one-spade opening. Your suit is worth no more as trump than in the previous example—the overcall is just as chancy. However, the great risk is now balanced by a great prospect of gain, and should be assumed.

Next, consider this example:

♠ K x x   ♡ K Q J 10 x x   ◊ J x   ♣ x x

Your magnificent suit makes an overcall safe at almost any level. Therefore, it would not be wrong to bid one heart over one diamond, or two hearts over one spade. However, this hand does not really meet the first test of an overcall—you do not have an opening bid. Here, you should consider using a *jump* overcall instead; we will see in the next chapter that most hands with only 1½ Quick Tricks are better treated in this fashion.

Remember that an overcall has not proven to be safe merely because it escapes an immediate penalty double; this is the primary risk, but the auction is not over. Your partner may take action of his own, expecting you to have a generous supply of high cards—he may try for game, or double the opponents. Then you will find that the initial safety given by a strong trump suit was an illusion. In the subsequent auction, it is a firm high-card structure which insures against disaster.

Vulnerability

Vulnerability can be a factor in deciding whether to overcall, but not such a big one as is popularly supposed. True, the possible loss is greater when you are vulnerable, but so is the gain if you have a game. If you stay out of the auction and defeat an enemy part-score contract 50 or 100 points when you could have made a vulnerable game, you have suffered a loss of over 500 points. The losses which come through bidding—the 500 and 800 sets— are more palpable and probably more irritating to partner, but they are no more real than the losses which come through passing.

Still, the odds are affected by unequal vulnerabilities. If you are vulnerable and the opponents are not, a 2– or 3-trick set will be a lot more than the value of the enemy game. And the opponents will be prone to double. So resolve any doubt in favor of passing. In contrast, when you are non-vulnerable against vulnerable opponents, you are in such good competitive position that you can afford to lower your normal standards slightly.

Two Suiters

There is one type of distributional holding which should induce you to strain to find an overcall—the possession of *two* long suits. An overcall with a two-suiter has twice the safety, since you can run to your second suit if doubled in the first. What is more, your game prospects are greatly enhanced by this distribution; a surprising number of tricks can be won when you have 6–5 or 5–5 pattern and partner has length in one of your suits. Of course, if your side has a good fit in some suit, the opponents have a good fit of their own elsewhere. And this is another compelling reason to enter the auction with a two-suiter—these deals often yield makeable high contracts for North-South and East-West both.

The hand below does not meet the requirements we have set up for an overcall:

♠ A Q x x x   ♡ x x   ◇ x   ♣ K 10 x x x

You do not have an opening bid in most styles; you have only a shabby suit to bid so there is risk, and you have on 2 Quick Tricks so there seems little chance for game. But you should bid one spade over a one-diamond or one-heart opening. The second suit in reserve gives you extra safety and extra game prospects as well.

With a two-suiter, generally bid the higher-ranking suit first. You may well bid both suits, and when you show the lower-ranking one second, partner can choose without increasing the level. This can hold true even when the lower-ranking suit is longer:

♠ A K x x x   ♡ K Q x x x x   ◇ x   ♣ x

Overcall one *spade* after a minor suit opening bid. It would be perfect to bid hearts and then bid and rebid spades, showing your 5–6 distribution. However, this can be done only against idealized opponents who never open their mouths; flesh and blood opponents will have the auction up to the three- or four-level before it gets back to you. So arrange your bidding to be able to show both of your suits conveniently.

Once in a while, convenience will dictate bidding the *lower* suit first. Over a one-heart opening bid, you hold:

♠ A Q 10 x x   ♡ Void   ◇ x x   ♣ A K x x x x

Bid two clubs. Half the time, the auction will be up to four hearts by your next turn; and then you can bid four spades. Had you overcalled one spade originally, you would have to bid five clubs over four hearts. And partner could not go back to four spades. The key factor is *not* that you have more clubs than spades; it is that only one of your suits is higher-ranking than the enemy suit. So you start with the lower, and bid the higher cheaply at whatever level is necessary. This is occasionally proper with a strong 5–5 two-suiter, and is usually so with 6–6.

One final reminder about two-suiters. If the opponents have bid *two* suits before it becomes your turn to act, and you hold the other two, do not overcall in either suit. Overcall in *both* at once by making a takeout double.

For the *freak* two-suiter, see page 65.

RESPONDING TO OVERCALLS

In general, respond to partner's overcalls as you do to his opening bids. If you would have passed an opening bid, pass after the overcall; but if you would have kept the auction alive had partner opened, give him the same courtesy when he overcalls. His hand, after all, may be very strong; and it should not be weak, since he did not employ the preemptive *jump* overcall.

Raising an Overcall

By far the most productive response to an overcall is a raise of partner's suit. If partner were anxious to hear about *your* suit, he would have doubled instead. And since an overcall usually is made in a long, strong suit, you are unlikely to find a better one for trump.

On this auction:

OPPONENT	PARTNER	OPPONENT	YOU
1 ♡	1 ♠	Pass	?

if you hold:

♠ 10 x x   ♡ x x x   ◊ A Q x x x   ♣ x x

Bid *two spades*. It would not be criminal to bid two diamonds instead, but it would be futile. If your side buys
this contract, you are going to play in spades—the only
question is *how high*—not *where* to play. So a two-diamond
response will serve only to complicate a simple auction.

What is more, the spade raise is better calculated to let
you buy the contract cheap if partner's overcall is minimum. Over two diamonds, opener could rebid two hearts,
and his partner might then be able to compete to three
hearts. But if you give an immediate raise to two spades,
opener is likely to be shut out. The raise of an overcall
always has considerable preemptive value. In fact, the
single raise is basically a semi-preemptive measure—intended as much to make trouble for the enemy as it is to
try for game. Its range is 5 to 8 points in support of partner's suit (add 1 point for each side doubleton, 3 points for
a singleton, 5 points for a void). Overcaller should pass the
raise unless his hand is worth 17 points or more.

Jump Raises

When you want to reach game opposite a 15– or
16-point overcall, that is when you have 9 to 11 points in
support, *jump* raise. If partner overcalls one heart after a
one-club opening, and you hold:

♠ x x x   ♡ K x x   ◊ A Q x x x   ♣ x x

Bid *three hearts*. You have 10 points in support of
hearts, counting the doubleton club, and that is far too
much for a single raise. Again, there is no reason to bid
diamonds; hearts will be your trump suit. The jump raise
conveys a simple message to partner: "Bid game with a
solid overcall, but pass with a minimum."

EXAMPLES

Partner should overcall one heart after a one-club opening with all three of these hands:

(a) ♠ x x   ♡ A Q J x x   ◇ J x x   ♣ A x x
(b) ♠ x x   ♡ A Q x x x   ◇ J x x   ♣ A K x
(c) ♠ x x   ♡ A Q J x   ◇ K x x   ♣ A K J x

With examples (a) and (b) he would pass a raise to two hearts, while with (c) he would try for game. After a *jump* raise, he would still pass with (a), but would go on to game with (b) and (c). Incidentally, notice the rare overcall in a four-card suit in example (c). This hand is too strong to pass, and has the wrong pattern for a takeout double; under these circumstances, an overcall in a strong four-card suit is usually the best solution. Partner will raise or jump-raise with three-card support, expecting greater length, but since a strong four-card suit plays very well opposite three-card support you will rarely be in trouble. Observe that if example (c) is faced by our earlier example of a jump raise, four hearts is the optimum contract despite the combined holding of only seven trumps.

Notrump Responses

There are many hands which lack three-card support for partner's overcall and yet call for some response. Even without a fit in partner's suit, you may make game facing an overcall if you have 7 or 8 points—partner may have a second suit, or overwhelming high-card strength. Thus, you must strain to give him a second chance to act, just as you would had he opened the bidding.

The response of one notrump to an overcall is a "courtesy" bid of this kind. It promises 6 or 7 to 10 points, and denies three-card or longer support for partner's major suit (if the overcall is one *diamond*, you may well try notrump even with support). Naturally, you must have some material in the enemy suit, but the quality of your stopper is not critical. This is because the one-notrump response is intended more to keep the auction alive than to make a serious try for a notrump game.

EXAMPLES

Bid:

OPPONENT	PARTNER	OPPONENT	YOU
1 ◇	1 ♠	Pass	*1 NT*

with these hands:

♠ x   ♡ J x x x   ◇ A Q x x   ♣ 10 x x x

♠ x x   ♡ K 10 x x x   ◇ Q x x   ♣ K x x

and even with:

♠ x x   ♡ K Q x x   ◇ 10 x x x   ♣ Q x x

The response of one notrump is quite desirable when you are unable to raise, for it limits your hand and allows partner to clarify his overcall. With a minimum, he can pass or rebid a very long suit; with a strong overcall, he can raise notrump or jump in his suit. And he can conveniently bid any second suit he holds, jumping in it if he has a powerful overcall.

The jump to *two* notrump in response to an overcall is highly invitational, but not forcing. It promises 11 or 12 points with a solid stopper in opener's suit (and most often two stoppers). Partner should bid game or force with a new suit when he has anything over minimum values for his overcall; but with nothing extra, partner will pass or sign off by rebidding his suit. On the auction above, jump to *two* notrump if you hold:

♠ K x   ♡ J x x x   ◇ A Q x x   ♣ Q x x

New Suit Responses

It is much less desirable to bid a new suit in response to an overcall than it is to raise or bid notrump. Raises and notrump responses have narrow point limits, so that partner can usually place the final contract with his rebid. In contrast, new suit responses are unlimited—the partnership is still groping for both the proper trump suit and level.

There can be three reasons for responding in a new suit.

(1) *A long, strong suit* which may well be better than partner's.

(2) *A scattering of points* which makes some response obligatory, when responder is without sufficient trump support for a raise and lacks even a semi-stopper in the enemy suit to justify a notrump response.

(3) *Sufficient strength* to guarantee game opposite a minimum overcall, and therefore enough to warrant slam investigation in case partner has a maximum.

EXAMPLES

OPPONENT	PARTNER	OPPONENT	YOU
1 ♣	1 ♡	Pass	1 ♠

This auction is proper with all three of these example hands:

(a) ♠ A Q J 10 x x   ♡ x x x   ◇ x x   ♣ x x
(b) ♠ A J x x   ♡ x x   ◇ K x x x   ♣ x x x
(c) ♠ A Q x x   ♡ K Q x x   ◇ A x x x   ♣ x

With example (a), you will rebid spades at your next turn. (If you held a king on the side, you would *jump* rebid next.)

With example (b), you will pass partner's next bid unless it is a jump. (With a king more, you would raise partner's second bid.)

With example (c), you will follow through with a diamond bid next, and finally with a jump in hearts. This will indicate your pattern and your slam ambitions.

Notice that the change of suit in response to an overcall (just like a response to an opening bid) has a very wide range in both strength and distribution, which must be clarified by responder's rebid. For this reason, it is *forcing;* overcaller must not let the auction die until you have had a chance to make the clarifying rebid. A one-heart response to a one-diamond overcall does not promise great strength, any more than would a one-heart response to a one-diamond *opening.* But both responses *may* be made with powerful hands. They are unlimited, and so cannot be passed.

After Two-Level Overcalls

So far, we have considered only responses to overcalls at the one-level. When partner bids at the two-level or higher, there is not so much room for delicate investigation. But even though the auction is crowded, all responses retain much the same meaning and limits that they have in answer to one-level overcalls.

Let us go back to two previous examples:

(a) ♠ x x x   ♡ 10 x x   ◊ A Q x x x   ♣ x x
(b) ♠ x x x   ♡ K x x   ◊ A Q x x x   ♣ x x

With (a), we raised a one-heart overcall to two hearts; with (b), we jumped to three hearts. Now suppose that the opening bid is one spade, and partner overcalls *two* hearts. With (a), raise to three hearts; with (b), jump to four hearts. True, you are forced to bid one level higher in each case; but partner needs a trick more to overcall at the two-level, so it comes out even.

Notrump responses are affected a little more by the increased level. If you would have jumped to two notrump over a one-level overcall, jump to *three* notrump over a two-level overcall. But you cannot answer a two-heart overcall with *two* notrump on all the hands with which you would have bid one notrump over *one* heart. The point-count requirement is the same—7 to 10—but your stopper in the enemy suit must now be secure, for there is much greater prospect of being raised to game in notrump.

Here is an example:

♠ J x x   ♡ Q x   ◇ J x x   ♣ A J x x x

If partner overcalls a one-diamond opening with one heart, you should respond one notrump. But if he over-calls a one-spade opening with two hearts, you may not respond two notrump—your stopper is insufficient. In-stead, bid three hearts! It is never pleasant to raise with a doubleton, but when partner overcalls at the two-level, he promises a suit which can stand such a raise. Even a small doubleton might do in a pinch.

The raise with a doubleton also eliminates the necessity to bid a *new suit* when you have a balanced hand with-out stoppers in the enemy suit. In response to a two-level overcall, you should bid a new suit only if it is likely to be better than partner's (this might be a five-card suit if it is a major and the overcall is in a minor; otherwise this means a strong six-card suit), or if you have a game-going or possible slam-going hand. Remember, the takeout to a new suit is unlimited and therefore forcing; it creates so much momentum that it must lead to a three– or four-level contract before either you or partner can stop.

Quiz

Left-hand opponent opens one spade, partner over-calls two hearts, next opponent passes, and it's up to you with these example hands. What do you bid?

(a) ♠ K Q 10   ♡ x x   ◇ A Q x x   ♣ Q x x x

(b) ♠ x x x   ♡ x x   ◇ Q x x   ♣ A K x x x

(c) ♠ Q x x x   ♡ Q x x   ◇ J x x   ♣ x x x

(a) *Three notrump.* Think of a two-level overcall as containing at least 14 or 15 points. If you can make game facing this much, bid it. You should bid *two* notrump without one of your queens.

(b) *Three hearts.* This asks partner to go on to game if he has a really strong overcall, 17 points or more. But partner, with the requisite strength, should bid four hearts only if he has a magnificent suit; otherwise he will try three notrump or show a second suit if possible.

(c) *Pass.* The overcall is not forcing. If partner could make game facing your hand, he is too strong to overcall.

THE IMMEDIATE CUE-BID

Requirements

A hand of 21 points or more is usually not suited to an overcall, for partner might well pass when game can be made. (Much the same is true of opening one-bids; here again the parallel between the opening bid and the overcall is useful.) For overly strong opening bids, you have the forcing two-bid; and if an opponent opens ahead of you when you were about to open with a two-bid, you look annoyed and then cue-bid—bid two of the enemy suit.

Responses

Your cue-bid is absolutely forcing—partner may not pass. What is more, every subsequent change of suit is forcing also, unless game has been reached. On this auction:

OPENER	YOU	RESPONDER	PARTNER
1 ♡	2 ♡	Pass	3 ♣
Pass	3 ♠	Pass	4 ♣
Pass	4 ◇	Pass	

partner was forced to bid over two hearts and over three spades; he is also forced to bid once more four diamonds. For the auction above, you might hold:

♠ A Q J x x x   ♡ x   ◇ A K J x x   ♣ A

Note that first-round control of the enemy suit is not obligatory. You may cue-bid with two small cards if the rest of your hand is strong enough.

Your cue-bid is *not* forcing to game, however. If at any point in the subsequent auction you raise partner, bid notrump, or rebid your suit, partner is invited—but not forced—to go on. With a worthless hand, he should pass on this auction:

OPENER	YOU	RESPONDER	PARTNER
1 ♡	2 ♡	Pass	2 ♠
Pass	3 ♠	Pass	?

For your bidding above, you might have:

♠ A K 10 x ♡ x ◇ A K Q J x ♣ A x x

If partner holds the queen of spades, a long spade suit, the ace of hearts, or a high club honor, he will go on. If *you* held anything extra (the queen of spades, for example) you would have bid four spades right over two spades.

If your hand were:

♠ A K x ♡ K Q 10 x ◇ A Q x x ♣ A x

you should, in the auction above, bid two notrump over partner's response. This is like a two-notrump opening bid; partner is urged to bid, but is allowed to pass. After all, you *could* have bid three notrump with more.

The third auction which gives partner a chance to pass is one like:

OPENER	YOU	RESPONDER	PARTNER
1 ♣	2 ♣	Pass	2 ♡
Pass	2 ♠	Pass	3 ◇
Pass	3 ♠	Pass	?

With game in your own hand, you should bid *four* spades at your third turn. To bid three spades, as above, you could hold:

♠ A K Q J x x ♡ Q x ◇ K Q J ♣ K Q

If partner has an ace or king, he will bid game; otherwise he will pass.

Freak Two-Suiters

There is one rare type of hand with which you would open a forcing two-bid as dealer, but which is better handled by a simple overcall, rather than a cue-bid, when an opponent opens. This is a freak two-suiter which has 15 points or fewer in high cards, a hand like:

♠ x   ♡ A K J 10 x x   ◊ A K 10 9 x x   ♣ Void

If your right hand opponent opens one club, bid *one heart*, not two clubs. It would be infuriating if everyone passed and left you in this unenterprising contract, but, believe me, it won't happen. When you have overwhelming *high card* strength, you subtract points from everyone at the table, and no one else may have a bid; but when your power is distributional, the points are still in the deck somewhere—and your freakish shape makes it *more* likely, not *less* likely, that someone else will find a bid and give you a second chance. The danger of the cue-bid— that your left-hand opponent will preempt or that opener will jump and rob you of the opportunity to bid both suits—far outweighs the danger of the simple overcall— that it will be passed out.

THE ONE-NOTRUMP OVERCALL

Requirements

The parallel between overcall and opening bid extends to the overcall of one notrump, for this describes a hand that you would have opened one notrump (the standard "strong" notrump of 16 to 18 points) had you been the dealer. Of course, the two one-notrump bids are not identical—an opponent's opening bid forces you to pay particular attention to stoppers in his suit before bidding notrump; and an opponent's opening makes one notrump a particularly dangerous bid to make.

When your one-notrump overcall is doubled, you are in serious trouble. You have a flat hand with no suit to run to, and any set will be a total loss since you have enough defense to prevent the enemy from making a high contract. What is worse, one notrump is by far the easiest overcall for the opponents to double. The opener's partner does not need length or strength in any one suit; whenever he has 8 points or more he can double for penalties, confident that his side has more high cards than yours.

Since the notrump overcall is riskier than the notrump opening (and has less to gain, as game prospects are dimmer after an enemy opening), why do you not need more strength for the bid? Actually, you do. But many balanced hands become stronger when an opponent opens ahead of you; your high cards lie behind your opponent's—your finesses will work. However, if you have a minimum one notrump opening which has *not* been improved by the enemy opening bid, avoid the notrump overcall. For example, suppose your right-hand opponent opens one heart and you hold one of these 16-point hands:

(a) ♠ A Q x   ♡ K J x   ◇ K 10 x x   ♣ K x x
(b) ♠ A x x   ♡ A x x   ◇ A x x x   ♣ A x x

Overcall one notrump with hand (a), for it is now worth nearly 18 points—your 4 points in hearts will probably take 2 tricks, and your holdings in all other suits have positional value. But do not overcall one notrump with hand (b), for your hand has not been improved by the opening. You have only one stopper, and no positional advantage. Not that you should pass over one heart. Use a takeout double, and pass partner's minimum response. Unless he can make a strong response, game cannot be made.

Responses

Responses to partner's one-notrump overcall are much the same as to a notrump opening—that is, responder places the contract. If you bid two of a new suit, this is where you intend to play the hand; you are signing off. If you want to be in a suit game, you jump right to it. If you wish to offer partner a choice between a suit game and three notrump, jump to three of your suit. In general, be a little optimistic, for the cards are well placed for you, and the fact that most of the enemy strength is concentrated in one hand is favorable. When in doubt, overbid.

This optimism should carry over into your notrump raises.

Jump to three notrump with 9 points or more.

Raise to two notrump with 7 or 8 points.

In short, look for only 25 points to bring home a game contract.

Stayman Convention

It is possible to check for a 4–4 fit in a major suit after partner's one-notrump overcall, but this is not necessarily done with the conventional (Stayman) two-club bid. You need this auction:

OPENER	PARTNER	RESPONDER	YOU
1 ◇	1 NT	Pass	2 ♣

to sign off in clubs (the fact that an opponent has opened makes it odds on that you will want to sign off; now that only three suits are available, it is more likely that clubs will be your suit). The conventional "Stayman" bid here is two *diamonds,* the cue-bid of opener's suit. This does not announce control of that suit, or in any way suggest slam. It asks partner to bid a four-card major suit if he has one, or to rebid two notrump if he hasn't. Regardless of what suit has been opened, the cue-bid of *that* suit asks partner to show an unbid four-card major. Only when the opening is one club is a response of two clubs to partner's one-notrump overcall the conventional Stayman inquiry for majors.

4

THE WEEK JUMP OVERCALL

♠   ♡   [◇]   ♣

WHEN TO JUMP

The takeout double and simple overcall are descriptive bids—they promise specific values and ask partner to bid on the basis of them. In contrast, the jump overcall is tactical, not descriptive—it is *not* intended to tell partner what sort of hand you hold, but rather to interfere with the enemy auction. Recently, I bid two *hearts* over an opponent's one-club opening bid holding:

♠ Q J 10 9 x x x   ♡ x x   ◇ x x   ♣ x x

Now, I am certainly not recommending this action to you. It was a bad bid which I thought might get a good result against these particular opponents (and it did); had it led to disaster, I was prepared to apologize abjectly to my partner (and you would never have heard about it). What I am trying to show is that the weak jump overcall is used primarily to prevent the opponents from getting to their best spot; only secondarily to get you to a good contract of your own.

The test of a jump overcall, then, is that you must believe that the enemy can make a higher contract than your side can, for otherwise you have used the weapon of preemption against yourself. Your game prospects must be dim, theirs bright. And this is a matter of high-card structure, of Quick Tricks.

Examples

A hand with 3½ Quick Tricks:

(a) ♠ A K J x x   ♡ x x   ◊ x x x   ♣ A Q x

will make a game facing as little as:

♠ Q x x   ♡ x x x x   ◊ x   ♣ K J x x x

and stop an opponent's game facing:

♠ Q x   ♡ x x x   ◊ J 10 x x x   ♣ J x x

In contrast, a hand with 1½ Quick Tricks:

(b) ♠ K J 10 9 x x   ♡ x x   ◊ A x x   ♣ x x

which has just about as much strength as hand (a), cannot make game even opposite:

♠ Q x x   ♡ A J x   ◊ K Q J x x   ♣ J x

In fact, the *opponents* might well make game against these two hands.

With hand (a), you are far more likely than the opponents to have a game, so you would overcall *one* spade; the opposite is true of hand (b), so you would overcall *two* spades.

Jump Overcall or Simple Overcall?

The dividing line falls at about 1½ to 2 Quick Tricks. With more than 2, you have too much chance for game and too much defense to preempt. With fewer than 1½ Quick Tricks, your high-card structure is too shaky for a simple overcall, for partner will bid games that go down or double the opponents in makable contracts; so, if you decide to overcall, you must jump. With 1½ or 2 Quick

Tricks, you can go either way, tending to jump with 1½, and to make a simple overcall with 2, but deciding each case on the basis of point-count, distribution, and tactics.

Quiz

(a) ♠ x x   ♡ A J 10 9 x x   ◇ K x x   ♣ x x

(b) ♠ x x   ♡ K Q J 10 x x   ◇ A x x   ♣ x x

(c) ♠ Q x   ♡ A K 10 x x x   ◇ Q 10 x x   ♣ x

(d) ♠ x x   ♡ A Q 10 x x   ◇ A x x x   ♣ x x

What do you bid with these hands if your right-hand opponent opens one club? What do you bid if he opens one spade?

(a) ♠ x x   ♡ A J 10 9 x x   ◇ K x x   ♣ x x

Jump to two hearts over one club. Your hand will take quite a few tricks on offense, but its high-card structure does not warrant a *one* heart overcall.

However, over a one *spade* opening bid, do not bid two hearts. If your hand does not qualify for a simple overcall at the one-level, it certainly doesn't at the two-level. Non-vulnerable, you might chance a jump overcall to three hearts. In unfavorable vulnerability, pass; *never make a simple overcall because you are not strong enough for a jump.*

(b) ♠ x x   ♡ K Q J 10 x x   ◇ A x x ♣ x x

If the opening is one club, this hand is borderline between a simple and a jump overcall. If you are *vulnerable,* it is better to concentrate on your own game prospects and bid one heart. However, non-vulnerable against vulnerable opponents, you might well jump in hearts, trying to push the enemy too high or to encourage partner to take a sacrifice. Likewise, if partner is a passed hand, use the jump overcall; your chance for game is slight, so concentrate on muddling up the opponents with a preempt.

If the opening bid is, instead, one spade, jump to three hearts on any vulnerability. This hand does qualify for a *two* heart bid, but it has neither the bright game prospects nor the solid defensive strength expected in a two-level overcall. Clearly, the best tactics is to go for the preemptive value of the jump.

(c) ♠ Q x ♡ A K 10 x x x ◇ Q 10 x x ♣ x

This hand, like example (b), has 2 Quick Tricks, but it is bolstered with fillers and excellent distribution. There is a reasonable chance for game if partner has a smattering of high cards, and the outlook on defense is not too gloomy. So the simple overcall, not the jump overcall, is called for.

Bid one heart over a one-club opening.

Bid two hearts over a one-spade opening.

(d) ♠ x x ♡ A Q 10 x x ◇ A x x x ♣ x x

Here, you have far less offensive strength than in any of the previous examples, but your high-card structure is better—2½ Quick Tricks. This improves your game prospects, and sharply decreases the enemy's. So bid one heart over a one-club opening.

If the opening bid is one spade, however, an overcall of *two* hearts becomes a poor risk. The great danger of a two-level overcall on such a broken suit outweighs the chance for game. So, pass. Do not even consider a jump to three hearts—you have exactly the wrong hand: defensive strength, offensive weakness. Just as you do not make a simple overcall because you are too weak to jump, you do not make a jump overcall merely because your hand does not qualify for a simple overcall. *Whether* you overcall at all is determined by suit strength, vulnerability conditions, and the level at which you must bid; *which* overcall you use is determined by high-card structure, Quick Tricks.

Strength Required

In the foregoing examples, jump overcalls were recommended for two hands. These hands are the tip-top upper limit of the preemptive jump (in fact, one of them qualifies as a simple overcall as well), not at all the usual holding for this action. The average jump overcall is considerably weaker, and some perfectly proper, if minimum, jumps bear no resemblance to those maximum hands. You might well bid two spades over a one-diamond opening with:

♠ K J 9 x x x   ♡ x   ◇ x x   ♣ 10 9 x x

or even, on favorable vulnerability, with:

♠ K Q J x x   ♡ x x   ◇ x x   ♣ x x x x

Non-vulnerable, particularly against vulnerable opponents, it is reasonable to jump to three clubs over one diamond, holding:

♠ x   ♡ J 10 x x   ◇ x x   ♣ Q J 10 x x x

Obviously, the weak jump overcall has a very wide range—from 3 to 10 high-card points, from 0 to 2 Quick Tricks. It is seldom possible for your side to bid accurately after the preemptive jump, for there is too much uncertainty about overcaller's strength. But you should lose very little by this, since the vast majority of these hands "belong" to the enemy. The jump overcall is designed to impede them, not to help you get to your best contract. And the uncertainty caused by the wide, hazy limits should hurt the opponents a great deal more than it hurts you.

RESPONDING TO THE JUMP OVERCALL

The key principle of responding to a jump overcall is simply expressed: ***Don't.*** Partner's preemptive jump does not invite you into the auction; it warns you to stay out. If partner bids two spades over a one-club opening, for example, he has taken a big risk. When your right-hand opponent fails to double him, partner has won his gamble; at no cost, he has robbed the opponents of two crucial levels of bidding. But if *you* now come into the auction, partner's neck is back on the block. So, in general, let the jump overcall do all the work for your side. If it crowds the enemy into a bad contract, you show a profit; if the opponents reach their normal spot, you break even. You cannot lose.

There are only two good reasons for bidding over partner's jump overcall—to increase the preemptive effect, or to try for game. The second reason is a rare one. It takes two opening bids facing each other to make game, and partner has considerably less than an opening bid (for otherwise he would have made a simple, not a jump, overcall). Therefore, you need at least an ace more than a minimum opening to think of game.

Examples

If partner jumps to two spades over a one-diamond opening, and you have any of these hands:

(a) ♠ x x ♡ A Q x x ◇ A x x x ♣ K x x
(b) ♠ K x ♡ Q J x x ◇ K J x x ♣ K Q x
(c) ♠ x ♡ K J x x ◇ A K x x ♣ K Q x x

Pass! Examples (a) and (b) would produce game opposite a simple overcall, but are too weak opposite a jump. Example (c) is strong enough, but the singleton spade argues for conservative action. The pass in this position actually has *aggressive* possibilities, for the enemy may reopen the auction and take a large penalty (particularly if you can manage to pass without devoting 30 seconds to vain regrets).

Going to Game

With $3\frac{1}{2}$ to 4 Quick Tricks and some support for partner's suit, you can start thinking about going to game. If partner jumps to two hearts over a one-club opening, bid four hearts holding:

♠ A x x   ♡ Q x   ◇ A K x x   ♣ A x x x

You can't be at all sure of making the contract, but it's worth trying. Even if the overcall is close to minimum, for example:

♠ Q x x   ♡ K J 10 x x x   ◇ x x x   ♣ x

there is an excellent play for game. But if your high-card structure or trump support is weaker, as in these examples:

♠ A x x   ♡ x x   ◇ A K x x   ♣ A x x x
♠ K x x   ♡ Q x   ◇ A K x x   ♣ K Q x x

you must not commit your side to game, for partner needs close to a maximum jump. Make a game *try*, by bidding a new suit—three diamonds or, if you wish, two spades. A change of suit is forcing, and asks overcaller either (1) to sign off with a minimum by rebidding his suit, or (2) to show a maximum by any other action, such as a jump to game in his own suit, a raise of *yours*, or a new suit bid. Note that you do *not* try for game by raising partner's overcall; as we will see, the raise is preemptive.

You may make game opposite a jump overcall with fewer than $3\frac{1}{2}$ Quick Tricks when you have good trump support and a side singleton or void. Suppose you hold:

♠ Q x x x   ♡ x   ◇ A Q 10 x   ♣ A x x x

If partner jumps to two spades over a one-club opening, you should raise to four spades. Naturally, you hope to make your game contract, but there is no way to tell in advance whether you will or not; it depends on partner's strength and fit. Why, then, don't you try for game rather than jump to it? Because if partner has a minimum jump overcall, a hand like:

♠ K J 10 x x x   ♡ J x x   ◇ J x   ♣ x x

so that your contract will go down (if the diamond king, as is likely, lies behind your ace), then the enemy can make game themselves. Your four-spade bid will get a maximum result no matter whether the diamond finesse loses or wins. If the king is on-side, you will make game; if it is off-side, you will take a profitable sacrifice.

Sacrificing

Whenever you have three– or four-card length in partner's suit and unbalanced distribution, this two-way action works for you. *If your side cannot make game, the enemy can.* So, jump to game regardless of your Quick Trick count. Bid four spades over a two-spade jump overcall with any of these hands:

(a) ♠ K x x x   ♡ x x x   ◇ A Q x x x   ♣ x

(b) ♠ A x x   ♡ x x x x   ◇ K J 10 x x x   ♣ Void

(c) ♠ A x x x   ♡ x   ◇ K J x x   ♣ x x x x

(d) ♠ Q x x x   ♡ A J 10 x x x   ◇ x   ♣ x x

In each of these cases, you are primarily taking a sacrifice. Of course, it is possible that partner has maximum high-card structure and the opponents cannot make a game because the cards lie wrong for them. But then the cards lie right for you, and your contract will be fulfilled.

When you hold one of these weaker hands opposite a jump overcall, it is likely that opener's partner will make a free bid. Do not let this stop you from raising; the fact that both opponents are in the bidding makes it *more* important to cut away their bidding room. On an auction like:

OPENER	PARTNER	RESPONDER	YOU
1 ♣	2 ♠	3 ♡	?

it is highly desirable to jump in spades when you have a good fit, regardless of your strength. Consider example (c) above:

♠ A x x x   ♡ x   ◇ K J x x   ♣ x x x x

If you pass over three hearts on this auction, opener will surely raise to four hearts. Of course, you can bid four spades now, but the belated sacrifice is much less effective. Suppose the whole hand is:

RESPONDER

♠ K J
♡ A Q x x x x
◇ x x x
♣ x x

PARTNER		YOU
♠ Q 10 9 x x x		♠ A x x x
♡ x x		♡ x
◇ A x x		◇ K J x x
♣ x x		♣ x x x x

OPENER

♠ x
♡ K J 10 x
◇ Q 10 x
♣ A K Q J x

Look at the difference between these two bidding sequences:

1. OPENER	PARTNER	RESPONDER	YOU
1 ♣	2 ♠	3 ♡	4 ♠
5 ♡	Pass	Pass	Pass

2. OPENER	PARTNER	RESPONDER	YOU
1 ♣	2 ♠	3 ♡	Pass (or 3 ♠)
4 ♡	Pass	Pass	4 ♠
Pass	Pass	Double	

On the first auction, opener will almost surely bid five hearts; he cannot afford to conceal his heart support—he could well miss even a slam. But on the second auction, opener can comfortably pass the sacrifice bid around to responder for he has already shown his fit, and responder has denied slam interest. The difference is 350 points—

four spades doubled down two, against five hearts down one. Three hundred points is a cheap price to pay to stop game, but it is much more satisfactory to be plus.

The general principle is to take any sacrifice immediately before the enemy have had room to exchange information. *Bid at once as high as you are willing to go.* Do not let them find their proper level and then offer them a choice between doubling you and going on.

EXAMPLES

Let us see how this principle is applied in a few examples:

♠ x x x	♡ J 10 x x x	◇ K x x x	♣ A
OPENER	PARTNER	RESPONDER	YOU
1 ♣	2 ◇	2 ♠	?

Bid five diamonds! You will have to take a sacrifice eventually, so do it immediately when it will have maximum effect. Why not pass first to see whether the opponents bid game? Because you know from your scanty defensive strength that they have a game, and they will know it too, looking at their own cards. If you put your head in the sand and pass, their game won't disappear.

♠ x	♡ A x x x	◇ x x	♣ Q J 10 x x x
OPENER	PARTNER	RESPONDER	YOU
1 ♠	3 ♡	3 ♠	?

Bid *five* hearts! The principle is the same in a major suit as in a minor—take your sacrifice immediately. Never bid four hearts and *then* five hearts; this is giving aid and comfort to the enemy.

♠ x x	♡ K Q x x x	◇ Void	♣ J 10 x x x x
OPENER	PARTNER	RESPONDER	YOU
1 ◇	2 ♡	3 ♡	?

Jump to *six* hearts at least! The opponents can probably

make a small slam, and possibly even a grand slam. Cut away all their bidding room and force them to guess at the seven-level by bidding *at once* as high as you are willing to go. A case could be made for a jump all the way to *seven* hearts, for fear that the opponents might bid and make seven spades if you leave them the six-level for investigation. Certainly any lesser bid than six hearts is a puny effort.

Raising

The single raise of a jump overcall may sound like very dull action after these glamorous leaps to five, six or seven, but it can be a very useful bid. On this sort of auction:

OPENER	PARTNER	RESPONDER	YOU
1 ◇	2 ♠	Pass	3 ♠

you are not trying for game—partner is barred from bidding again. If you wished to suggest game, you would have bid a new suit. What are you doing, then? You are bidding at once as high as you are willing to go. For the auction above, you might hold any of these hands:

(a) ♠ K x ♡ A x x ◇ Q 10 x x ♣ K Q x x
(b) ♠ x x x ♡ K J x x ◇ A x x ♣ A x x
(c) ♠ Q x x ♡ A K x ◇ x x ♣ Q J 10 x x

Notice that you do not want to be in four spades with any one of these examples, either trying to make game or as a sacrifice. Then why jeopardize the part-score by raising to three? You raise because opener may come back into the auction. With hand (c), you are trying to keep the enemy out; they may even have a game, but you cannot sacrifice profitably at the four-level.

With hand (b), you are competing for a part-score. Probably both sides can make contracts at the three-level, but you will be happy to defend at the four-level. Rather than let the enemy exchange information and *then* bid three spades, you bid it right away for maximum effect.

With hand (a), you are confident of making three spades, and anxious to double any enemy contract at the four-level. Your best chance is to try to push the opponents into doubling range before they limit their hands.

However, avoid the single raise when responder has made a forcing free bid over the jump overcall.

OPENER	PARTNER	RESPONDER	YOU
1 ♣	2 ♡	2 ♠	3 ♡

This is a futile action. It cannot push the opponents too high, for it gives opener a chance to pass with a minimum opening while otherwise he would have to bid. And it does not impede the enemy, for opener can show a strong hand or a good fit by bidding freely. In this position, you should either jump in hearts or pass. The "half-way" action helps the opponents, not you.

In summary, then, do not bid at all over partner's jump overcall unless you have close to 4 Quick Tricks or strong distributional support. With a good fitting hand, make the highest bid you can afford, and then retire from the auction. *Never push the opponents into a high contract and then sacrifice.*

HIGHER JUMP OVERCALLS

Bidding at once as high as you are willing to go applies to overcalls as well as to responses. When you have made a jump overcall, you are out of the auction from then on (unless partner invites you back in by forcing with a new suit); you have done your all. A sequence like:

OPENER	YOU	RESPONDER	PARTNER
1 ♡	2 ♠	3 ◊	Pass
3 ♡	3 ♠		

is criminal. You have allowed the opponents to exchange information and then given them another crack at you. If you were willing to be in three spades on your own, you should have bid *three* spades right over one heart and made the enemy guess what to do.

Double Jump Overcalls

The *double* jump overcall is made on a more freakish pattern hand than is the single jump. You usually have at least a seven-card suit, and a side singleton or void. As with the single jump, your high-card structure does not warrant a simple overcall; were you the dealer, you would not open with a one bid (although you might well open with three). Bid three spades over a one-club opening, holding:

♠ Q J 10 x x x x	♡ x	◇ Q J x x	♣ x
♠ K Q J x x x x	♡ x	◇ Q 10 x	♣ x x

The double-jump overcall is made with the sort of hand that suggests a profitable sacrifice against an opponent's game contract. Therefore, partner is expected to take a sacrifice (immediately, as over the single jump) unless he expects to defeat the enemy contract. This sort of auction:

OPENER	YOU	RESPONDER	PARTNER
1 ◇	3 ♠	4 ♡	Pass
Pass	4 ♠		

is sheer folly. Partner knows what your hand looks like and you can have no conception of his, so it is up to *him* to take any sacrifice. His pass over four hearts means that in his informed judgment a sacrifice is wrong: he may be able to defeat four hearts (but not any other game, so he did not double); he may be sure that the sacrifice will be too expensive; he may know that the enemy can make a slam. To put it another way, your three-spade preempt has forced the opponents to guess at their proper contract. Only your partner knows whether they guessed right or wrong.

However, if you now sacrifice, the opponents cannot

have guessed wrong. If they have underbid or bid the wrong suit, they have a chance to correct; if they have overbid, they can double you. Never give the enemy two shots at you by preempting and then bidding again. If your own hand demands a four-spade sacrifice, jump right to four spades over the opening bid and make the opponents guess at the five-level before they have exchanged information.

Triple Jump Overcalls

This triple jump should always be based on a freak distributional hand—an eight-card suit, or a two-suiter. Bid four hearts over a one-diamond opening with:

| ♠ x x | ♡ K Q J x x x x x | ◇ x | ♣ A x |
| ♠ x | ♡ A K J x x x x | ◇ x | ♣ Q J x x |

If partner has a little strength in the right places you may make your contract; otherwise you are sacrificing. Note that either hand would qualify for a *one*-heart overcall. But with so much offense and so little defense, you should do your best to destroy the opponents' communications. What should you do with either hand above on this auction?

OPENER	YOU	RESPONDER	PARTNER
1 ◇	4 ♡	4 ♠	Pass
Pass	?		

You must *pass*. Partner knows you have a freak, and it is *his* responsibility to sacrifice, not yours.

THE UNUSUAL NOTRUMP OVERCALL

It is sometimes possible to make a preemptive jump overcall in *two* suits at once by using the "unusual notrump." This is an artificial device—it announces not a balanced, notrump type hand, but a freakish two-suiter in clubs and diamonds, the minor suits.

When an Overcall Is Unusual

When is a notrump overcall "unusual" instead of natural? There are four "unusual" situations:

(1) Any direct notrump overcall by a passed hand. (A player who could not open the bidding obviously cannot have the 16 points or more needed for the natural notrump overcall.)

(2) Any *jump* overcall to two notrump. (Since a *one*-notrump overcall is available to show the 16 to 18 point hand, and a takeout double or cue-bid can be made with any greater strength, the *two*-notrump overcall is an unnecessary, and thus an unusual, bid.)

(3) An overcall in notrump directly over an opponent's notrump bid. (If an opponent bids notrump and you have a very strong hand, you would double. If you bid *two* notrump over a one-notrump opening, for example, you are using the unusual notrump.)

(4) A notrump overcall when the opponents have shown strong hands, and are obviously going to game or slam. (An opponent has opened a strong two-bid; or opener's partner has responded with a jump shift or a jump raise. You could not expect to fulfill a notrump contract against such strength, so a notrump overcall is unusual.)

Thus, if an opponent deals and opens one heart or one spade and you jump to two notrump over the opening, you have a freak hand with length in both clubs and diamonds, not a strong balanced hand. But on this auction:

OPENER	PARTNER	RESPONDER	YOU
1 ♡	Pass	2 ♡	2 NT

your notrump overcall is natural, not unusual—you have

made the cheapest available bid to show a strong, balanced hand. Only if you are a passed hand:

YOU	OPENER	PARTNER	RESPONDER
Pass	1 ♠	Pass	2 ♠
2 NT			

is a non-jump notrump overcall unusual. Now there is no need for the natural strong meaning, so the bid becomes artificial. And if responder had bid *three* spades, a three notrump overcall would be unusual whether or not you had passed originally.

Requirements

To use the unusual notrump overcall, you should have at least ten cards in the minor suits, normally five or more in each. You do not promise any minimum high-card content; the more freakish your distribution, the fewer points you need.

These are all reasonable hands for an unusual notrump:

(1) ♠ x   ♡ x x   ◊ K Q J x x   ♣ K J 10 x x
(2) ♠ x   ♡ x   ◊ A J 10 x x   ♣ Q J 10 x x x
(3) ♠ Void   ♡ x   ◊ K J x x x x   ♣ Q 10 x x x x

Notice that these are not strong hands; not one of them qualifies for an opening bid. The unusual notrump overcall is not a try for game—it is an attempt to find a profitable sacrifice or to crowd the opponents into a poor contract. When you hold a *strong* two-suiter in the minors, for example:

♠ x   ♡ A x   ◊ K Q J x x   ♣ K J 10 x x

make a simple overcall. Over a one-spade opening, bid two diamonds, intending to show the clubs later, if convenient. A two-*notrump* overcall might encourage partner to sacrifice against a game contract that the opponents could not make, or discourage partner from trying for a notrump or heart game that your side *could* make.

You may, if you wish, make use of the unusual notrump with a powerful hand when you have really wild distribution.

Holding:

♠ x   ♥ Void   ♦ A K J x x x   ♣ K Q J x x x

it is conceivable action to jump to two notrump over a major-suit opening, intending to raise partner's minor suit response to game. However, this is an *unusual* unusual notrump; partner will not expect you to have such great high-card strength. Even with this freak hand, you might well do better, in the long run, making a simple two-diamond overcall, and following through with a five-club bid next. In case the auction sky-rockets to the five– or six-level, partner will then know that you have some defense against a high enemy contract; that you have high cards, not merely distribution. The unusual notrump overcall is normally used with hands that appear to belong to the opponents, not to you. It is a *preemptive* jump overcall.

Responding to the Unusual Notrump

PREFERENCE

When partner makes an unusual notrump overcall, treat it much as you would any other preemptive jump overcall. Of course, you may not pass unless there is an intervening bid. You are obliged to choose between partner's two suits. But the auction:

OPENER	PARTNER	RESPONDER	YOU
1 ♥	2 NT	Pass	3 ♣ (or
			3 ♦)

means that you would have *passed* had partner jumped to three clubs or three diamonds over the opening bid. For the auction above, you might well hold:

♠ K J x x   ♥ K x x   ♦ x x   ♣ 10 x x

Conceivably, you could hold only a doubleton club—you are taking a preference between partner's suits, not bidding a suit of your own.

JUMP RESPONSE

When you would have raised a jump overcall in one of the minor suits, either in an attempt to make game or as a sacrifice, *jump* in response to the unusual notrump. You are in excellent position to evaluate the offensive potential of your side. High cards in clubs and diamonds are priceless for offense; four-card support for either minor is almost enough in itself to warrant a jump, and length in one minor suit combined with shortness in the other is a powerful combination. The only values in spades or hearts which count for offense are aces or voids—first-round controls.

Likewise, you can estimate your side's defensive strength very closely. In the minor suits, only aces are sure tricks, although shortness in clubs or diamonds suggests that partner may provide a trick or two on defense. Honors and length in the *major* suits are the real measure of defensive potential. Consider these two hands:

(a) ♠ A x x x   ♡ x x x   ◇ K x   ♣ K J x x
(b) ♠ K J 10 x   ♡ Q J x   ◇ x x   ♣ A x x x

They have identical distribution and point-count, but are poles apart in both offensive and defensive strength when partner jumps to two notrump over an enemy one-heart opening bid. Hand (a) is powerful for offense, since all of its high cards are working, but weak for defense. Hand (b) is of some use offensively because of the four-card club support and the doubleton diamond, but its high cards are primarily defensive. Suppose partner holds, for his unusual notrump overcall:

♠ x   ♡ x   ◇ A J x x x x   ♣ Q 10 9 x x

With hand (a), you are an overwhelming favorite to make

five clubs, but are unlikely to set an enemy game contract in either major. With hand (b), you have to be lucky to make *three* clubs, but can surely defeat any opposing game contract one or two (or even three) tricks. Therefore, with hand (b) you should make the "negative" takeout to three clubs over two notrump; with hand (a), you should make a "positive" response—a jump in clubs.

How high do you jump? The principle is the same as in responding to any other preemptive overcall—bid at once as high as you are willing to go. If you intend to sacrifice in five of a minor, or if you hope to make game, jump right to five over two notrump. When you are willing to let the opponents play in four of a major—either because a sacrifice would be too expensive or because you expect to defeat them—you jump to four clubs or four diamonds.

EXAMPLES

On this auction:

OPENER	PARTNER	RESPONDER	YOU
1 ♠	2 NT	Double	?

What would be your action with each of these example hands:

(a) ♠ K x x ♡ Q 10 x x x x ◇ x x ♣ J x

(b) ♠ K J x x ♡ Q 10 x x ◇ K x ♣ 10 x x

(c) ♠ A J 10 x ♡ Q J x x x ◇ x ♣ K x x

(d) ♠ x x x ♡ A J x x x ◇ Q x x x ♣ x

(e) ♠ x x x ♡ x ◇ A J x x x ♣ K 10 x x

(a) ♠ K x x ♡ Q 10 x x x x ◇ x x ♣ J x

Pass. If responder had not doubled, you would have had to bid three clubs. However, you are no longer forced to choose between the minors, for partner will get a chance to bid his better suit himself.

(b) ♠ K J x x ♡ Q 10 x x ◇ K x ♣ 10 x x

Bid three clubs. Here you have a real preference for clubs, and it is your duty to show it. This bid should not encourage partner to sacrifice later on; he has shown his hand, and subsequent action is up to you.

(c) ♠ A J 10 x ♡ Q J x x x ◇ x ♣ K x x

Bid four clubs. Your good club support, singleton diamond, and side ace should give you a fine play for your contract if the opponents double you. And if they bid four of a major suit instead, you are prepared to double *them*. Note that you are not inviting partner to sacrifice; you are bidding at once as high as you believe your partnership should go. Of course, if partner has really extreme distribution (such as two six-card suits) he will bid five clubs; but then you will have a play for your contract.

(d) ♠ x x x ♡ A J x x x ◇ Q x x x ♣ x

Bid five diamonds. You are unlikely to fulfill your contract, but the sacrifice should be inexpensive. Surely, you are unwilling to let the opponents play four spades. By sacrificing prematurely, you may push the enemy into a five– or six-level contract which you can defeat.

(e) ♠ x x x ♡ x ◇ A J x x x ♣ K 10 x x

Bid six diamonds. Your hand fits so well with partner's that heroic measures are in order—the enemy have a hand-in-glove fit also, and can make practically whatever they bid. Don't give them room to find this out for themselves; at this stage, only *you* know that they can make five or six hearts.

It is obvious from the foregoing that virtually the entire responsibility for sacrificing rests upon the *partner* of the unusual notrump bidder. If you have used the unusual notrump properly, you have described a hand with great offensive possibilities in clubs and diamonds, but with little defense against hearts and spades. It is almost always wrong to rebid these same values by sacrificing later. Only partner knows whether the enemy game contract can make, whether your sacrifice will be cheap or expensive. True, you are a better player than he is, but in this instance you must let him make the final decision nevertheless.

A Warning

Finally, a word of warning about the unusual notrump: this device has caused more disastrous confusion in bidding than all the other conventional bids combined. On two occasions, famous experts playing in World Championship matches have had costly disagreements over whether a notrump overcall was "unusual" or not. And in less august circles, the mix-ups have been countless.

If you are a passed hand, you cannot be strong enough for a natural notrump overcall.

A jump to two notrump is unnecessary as a natural bid.

A natural notrump overcall directly over an enemy notrump bid is absurd.

And a natural notrump overcall after the opponents have shown the values for a game or slam is impossible.

So in these four situations, the notrump overcall is unusual. But *only* in these four situations. Most notrump overcalls are natural. Unless you are a passed hand, any non-jump notrump overcall is natural unless the opponents have shown great power. The immediate overcall of *three* notrump is natural. An original notrump overcall *can* be unusual, but not a notrump response or rebid. The overriding principle is that when your notrump overcall has a sensible, natural interpretation, then that is what it means. Only if it is meaningless is it unusual.

If you have to worry what the bid means every time you or your partner bids notrump, then give up the unusual notrump. You will not get enough freak two-suiters in the minors to make up for an occasional disastrous misunderstanding.

5

TRAPPING AND BALANCING

♠　♡　◇　♣

TRAPPING

It is not possible to double an opening suit bid for penalties. When you hold a powerful hand with length and strength in the suit opened, your best action is usually to pass. This is snake-in-the-grass tactics; you hope that the auction will develop in such a fashion that you can later double and collect a fat penalty.

Trap Pass

With each of these hands below you should "trap" pass over an enemy one-spade opening bid:

(a) ♠ K J x x x　♡ A x　◇ K Q x　♣ K x x
(b) ♠ Q J 9 x x x　♡ K J x　◇ A K　♣ x x
(c) ♠ A Q 10 x　♡ A K x x　◇ Q J x x ♣ x

Should the auction then go:

OPENER	YOU	RESPONDER	PARTNER
1 ♠	Pass	1 NT	Pass
Pass	?		

or

OPENER	YOU	RESPONDER	PARTNER
1 ♠	Pass	1 NT	Pass
2 ♠	?		

you will spring your trap and double for penalties. This sort of double is *not* cooperative; partner must leave it in regardless of how weak he is. Therefore, you must have the expectation of taking at least six defensive tricks in your own hand. And your strength must not be concentrated mainly in trumps, for you must reckon with the possibility that responder may run to a new suit and your partner might double *that*.

When Not to Double

With either of these hands:

(d) ♠ K J x x x   ♡ x x   ◊ K x x   ♣ K x x
(e) ♠ Q J 9 x x x   ♡ x x x   ◊ A Q x   ♣ x

do *not* double on the example auctions above. With hand (d), you cannot be sure of defeating the contract if partner is weak. With hand (e), you have defense only against a spade contract; so do not drive the enemy into a makable spot. In neither case can the hand "belong" to your side, since partner did not act independently over one notrump. So be satisfied with a small profit if you can get one.

Do not double even with the strong hands—examples (a), (b) and (c)—when responder shows strength with a two-over-one takeout.

OPENER	YOU	RESPONDER	PARTNER
1 ♠	Pass	2 ♣	Pass
2 ♠	?		

Partner surely has the prettiest bust you ever saw, so pickings will be lean at the two-level. And the opponents may well bid higher if you do not warn them off. Be patient and pass again.

Delayed Double

Patience is required also when opener rebids in a new suit:

OPENER	YOU	RESPONDER	PARTNER
1 ♠	Pass	1 NT	Pass
2 ♣			

you can double at this point only with a hand like example (c).

(c) ♠ A Q 10 x ♡ A K x x ◇ Q J x x ♣ x

Your double is for takeout on this auction, a three-suit takeout double of clubs, forcing partner to bid at the two-level. You expect partner to bid hearts or diamonds but he may bid spades if he wishes, for you promise spade strength behind the bidder. Partner is encouraged to convert your takeout into a penalty double by passing whenever he has club length.

You *may not* employ this delayed takeout double with hands (a) or (b), repeated below:

(a) ♠ K J x x x ♡ A x ◇ K Q x ♣ K x x
(b) ♠ Q J 9 x x x ♡ K J x ◇ A K ♣ x x

It is most irritating to have to pass again, but you must. If you double, partner is odds on to bid your short suit—partners are like that—and you may be in serious trouble despite your strength. This looks like a misfit hand in which neither side can make anything, so let the enemy go down instead of you. And if two clubs turns out to be the opponents' perfect spot, tough luck. After all, the enemy, too, is entitled to get a good result now and then.

REOPENING THE AUCTION

A trap pass is made in the hope that responder will act over the opening bid, and that the enemy will land in serious trouble. But half the time, opening bidder's partner will not have enough strength to respond, and will pass. If fourth hand passes also, your side may get a filthy result—you may even miss game, and collect a measly 100 or 150 points instead.

Therefore, if *you* are fourth hand, and in the pass-out position on an auction like:

OPENER	PARTNER	RESPONDER	YOU
1 ♡	Pass	Pass	?

you must make a determined effort to keep the bidding alive, even with scanty values.

Suppose on the auction above you hold:

♠ x x x   ♡ x   ◇ x x x   ♣ A J 10 x x x

You should reopen with two clubs! Why bid with only 5 high-card points after partner has passed? Partner is marked with a strong hand—perhaps the best hand at the table—just as surely as if he had doubled or overcalled; for where are the 40 points in the deck? Give opener 16 high-card points, an ace better than a minimum opening, and give responder 4 points for his pass, close to maximum. Still, partner has 15 points, and he may well have more. Clearly he passed over one heart because he was long in hearts, not because he was weak. At the very least, he has a sound opening bid, and would you let the opponents buy the hand at the one-level if your partner had opened the bidding?

Bidding partner's cards in the reopening position is known as "balancing"; that is, you presume that partner has the balance of strength which the opponents tell you they don't have, and which is not in your hand. Doubles, overcalls and jump overcalls change drastically in meaning when they are used in the pass-out, "balancing" position.

Your first duty in the balancing position is to tell partner why you are bidding: Are you bidding his cards, or do you have real values of your own? If your bid is based on values partner must hold, you balance with an overcall. If you might have doubled or overcalled right over the opening bid (had you been in second seat), you normally reopen with a double, regardless of your distribution.

Reopening Doubles

This reopening double has a value beyond that of describing a good hand: if partner was "trapping" over the opening bid, he can pass your takeout double for penalties. This will yield a juicy set even at the one-level, for when partner is trapping and you have enough strength to double, your side has the bulk of the high cards, with trumps massed behind declarer. Opener is in serious trouble. Thus, it is very desirable to reopen with a double whenever your high-card content will support a penalty pass. But you must not double with a weak hand, for then if partner passes you will not get a satisfactory result from the one-level doubled contract.

REQUIREMENTS

The dividing line is 10 points in high cards—an average hand. With 10 points or more, you may reopen with a double; with fewer, you may not.

The balancing takeout double does not, then, have the normal rigid distributional requirements. It guarantees not support for all unbid suits, but enough high cards to tolerate a penalty pass or produce game if partner is trapping.

EXAMPLES

If a one-diamond opening bid by your left-hand opponent is passed around to you, double with all three of these hands:

(a) ♠ K J x x   ♡ Q 10 x x   ◇ K x   ♣ A J x

(b) ♠ x x   ♡ A K Q x x   ◇ x x   ♣ K J x x

(c) ♠ A x x   ♡ A x x   ◇ x x x   ♣ Q x x x

Notice that these examples are quite dissimilar. If the one-diamond opening were at your *right*, you would double with (a), overcall with (b), and pass with (c). In the pass-out position, however, you must double with them all and then distinguish among them by your rebid. Suppose partner answers one spade. You should raise to two spades with (a), confirming a normal takeout double. You should rebid two hearts with (b), indicating that what you really hold is an overcall. You should pass with (c), for you doubled only in case partner was trapping.

RESPONSES

When partner uses this wide-range reopening double, how do you respond? Since you have passed over the opening bid, you cannot hold a powerful hand unless you have length in the enemy suit. If you were trapping with a strong opening bid of your own, you can safely pass the double for penalties, or, particularly vulnerable against non-vulnerable, jump in notrump. And when you passed over the opening because you were too weak to act, simply bid your best suit (or notrump) at a minimum level, and await partner's clarifying rebid. Do not jump in response, even with ten or eleven points; if partner would have acted in the *direct* position, he will rebid. And then you can either try for game or pass, according to whether you have a fairly good or a poor hand.

Quiz

OPENER	YOU	RESPONDER	PARTNER
1 ♡	Pass	Pass	Double
Pass	?		

What do you bid with these examples:

(a) ♠ K x   ♡ K Q 10 x   ◇ A J x x x   ♣ K x

(b) ♠ J x x   ♡ K x x   ◇ A Q x x x   ♣ x x

(c) ♠ Q x x   ♡ Q J x   ◇ J 10 x x   ♣ x x x

(a) Pass for penalties—this is what you hoped for when you trapped over the opening. However, vulnerable against non-vulnerable, jump to three notrump, as the set may not compensate you for the sure vulnerable game.

(b) Bid two diamonds. If partner passes, you will have missed nothing. If he bids again, you will then try for a notrump (or spade, if that is partner's rebid) game.

(c) Bid one notrump and pass partner's rebid. Try to avoid responding in a weak four-card suit, since partner may not have support.

Reopening Overcalls

If you are not strong enough to reopen with a double (that is, if you have 9 points or fewer) you can "balance" with an overcall. If a one-diamond opening bid is passed around to you in fourth seat, overcall in your long suit with each of these hands:

♠ A Q x x x   ♡ x x   ◇ x x   ♣ J 10 x x

♠ J x x x   ♡ K 10 x x x   ◇ x   ♣ A x x

♠ K x   ♡ x x x   ◇ x x   ♣ Q J 10 x x x

Note that not one of them qualifies for a *direct* overcall; if you were that good, you would double. A reopening overcall means that you would have passed (or possibly jumped preemptively) if the opening bid had been at your right. You promise a five-card suit—possibly a strong four-carder at the one-level—and little else.

Partner, therefore, is not supposed to get too enthusiastic. Even when he was trapping with a strong hand, game is unlikely. He needs a good fit and 16 points or more even to consider game possibilities. Normally, he should realize that you are merely competing for a part-score, and pass your overcall.

Reopening Jump Overcalls

What is the reopening *jump* overcall? Obviously, it is no longer needed as a preemptive device; you don't have to worry about the opponents. The simple overcall describes your distributional hands which are light in high cards. Therefore, the jump overcall can be used to describe a fairly strong hand (about 10 or 12 points) which is unsuitable for a reopening double.

Suppose your left-hand opponent opens one heart, and this is passed around to you. You hold:

♠ x x x   ♡ x x   ◊ J x   ♣ A K Q 10 x x

You are strong enough to double, but if partner passes for penalties you are unlikely to get a satisfactory result. Your values are offensive, not defensive; you want to play three notrump if partner is trapping, not one heart doubled. Further, what will you do if partner responds two diamonds to your double? If you pass you are in the wrong spot; if you bid three clubs, *over partner's two diamonds,* you describe a much stronger hand. So jump to three clubs right away.

On the auction above, these example hands are better suited to the reopening jump overcall than to the double:

♠ K Q J x x x   ♡ x   ◊ K J x x   ♣ x x
♠ K J x   ♡ Void   ◊ A Q 10 x x x x   ♣ x x x

Reopening One Notrump Overcalls

Another bid which changes its meaning in the "balance" position is the one-notrump overcall. This auction:

OPENER	PARTNER	RESPONDER	YOU
1 ♠	Pass	Pass	1 NT

does not describe a 16 to 18 point hand; you would double (and rebid in notrump) with that strength. It shows a hand just under the strength for a reopening double—8 or 9 points—which has no suit available for an overcall. For instance, this hand:

♠ K x   ♡ Q x x x   ◇ K J x x   ♣ x x x

is typical for the auction above. Why bid at all? Because if partner is trapping with 15 points or more, your side can probably make game. Note that the reopening, balancing notrump overcall does not promise substantial values in the enemy suit. *Partner* has length there; why else did he pass over the opening bid? He is known to have a reasonably strong hand, for the high cards are in the deck somewhere.

Like all reopening overcalls, one notrump warns partner not to try for game—it means that you have already bid most of *his* values. Only if partner has a lot more than the 12 or 13 points you expect, if he has 15 points or more, should he raise notrump. Of course, with an unbalanced hand partner should sign off at two of a suit; he need not pass one notrump if he dislikes that contract.

Passing Instead of Reopening

It is obvious, then, that you really go out of your way to keep the auction alive in the pass-out position. When partner has trap-passed, you may make a game with as little as 24 or 25 points in the combined hands, for almost all the enemy high cards are bottled up in one hand, and partner's strength lies behind it. In any event, the odds are that the hand belongs to your side, so why let them play it at the one-level?

PASS WEAK HANDS

Why? Well, one good reason might be that you are *so* weak that any bid would have to get you overboard. If you hold:

♠ 10 x x   ♡ Q x x x   ◇ Q x x   ♣ Q x x

you should not reopen in fourth seat, no matter what the opening bid was. If you bid one notrump, you will probably go down, because if partner has the 15 points you need to make *one* notrump, he will raise and you will go down at two or three notrump. So do not reopen with a balanced hand of seven points or fewer.

This has a corollary: partner must not "trap" with 18 points or more—obviously, he cannot then hope for a reopening double, and he must fear that you cannot reopen at all with some hands which will produce game.

DON'T BALANCE WITH LENGTH IN OPENER'S SUIT

The second good reason for passing in the "balancing" position is that you have length in opener's suit. On the auction:

OPENER	PARTNER	RESPONDER	YOU
1 ♠	Pass	Pass	?

pass with any of these hands:

(a) ♠ K J 10 x x   ♡ x x   ◇ A x x   ♣ x x x
(b) ♠ A J 10 x   ♡ A x x   ◇ Q x x   ♣ x x x
(c) ♠ Q J x x x   ♡ A K   ◇ A x x x   ♣ x x

Partner cannot be trapping with a strong hand and spade length, for there are not that many spades in the deck. Therefore, you cannot possibly have game with hands (a) and (b); by reopening, you trade the certainty of setting one spade for the doubtful chance of making a partial which may well be worth less than the penalty. Can you not miss game by passing with hand (c)—couldn't partner have 11 or 12 points? It is most unlikely, for partner is short in spades, and could have acted with any fair hand. Once again, take the sure profit. The more cards you have in the enemy suit, the less likely it is that partner has passed with a good hand, the more likely it is that you can set the opponents where they are, but make nothing yourself.

BALANCING LATER IN THE AUCTION

The same reasoning that leads you to reopen with light hands in the pass-out position—that partner must have the strength which the opponents deny holding—applies to many other bidding situations on the second or even third round of the auction. For example, consider this sequence:

OPENER	YOU	RESPONDER	PARTNER
1 ♡	Pass	2 ♡	Pass
Pass	?		

The opponents are unlikely to hold much more than half the high-card points in the deck. They have found a fit, and so each of them is doubtless counting extra points for distributional values; yet neither opponent could try for game. The average expectancy is to find opener with about 13 high-card points, and responder with about 7.

Balancing Overcalls

If you hold some hand such as, after the bidding sequence above:

♠ K J x x x   ♡ x x   ◇ K J x   ♣ x x x

you can count on partner to have from 10 to 12 points just as surely as if you were looking at his cards. Suppose the enemy hands are:

OPENER	RESPONDER
♠ A x x	♠ x x
♡ A Q x x x	♡ K J x x
◇ A x x	◇ x x x
♣ x x	♣ K J 10 x

Each of them is close to maximum for his action, but this still leaves partner with:

♠ Q x x   ♡ x x   ◊ Q x x x   ♣ A Q x x

Notice that the enemy can make two hearts, while you can make at least two spades. How do you get into the auction? By reopening the bidding—balancing—with two spades when opener passes two hearts! Here, again, you are bidding cards which you know to be in partner's hand.

The theory is that when the opponents have found a fit in their suit, your side has a fit in some other suit; if they have eight or nine hearts, you and partner have eight or nine clubs or diamonds or spades, almost invariably. And if they have stopped at a low contract despite their fit, you and partner must have enough high cards to compete effectively. Although neither of you has enough to warrant an independent bid, the auction tells you that you have enough strength *together* to make reopening action safe and profitable. (Even if you cannot make a two– or three-level contract, you are likely to push the enemy to the three-level and defeat *them*.)

Balancing Doubles

Look again at the two hands cited earlier:

(a)	(b)
♠ K J x x x	♠ Q x x
♡ x x	♡ x x
◊ K J x	◊ Q x x x
♣ x x x	♣ A Q x x

If the opponents pass out at two hearts after finding a fit, you would "balance" with a two-spade bid if you held hand (a), deducing that partner held a hand like (b). What would you do, though, if you held hand (b) in the balancing position? You could still presume that your side has nearly half the points and a trump fit somewhere, but now you have no suit to reopen with. Therefore, you would *balance with a takeout double*. (Partner, if he holds hand (a), will then bid two spades in response.)

On this sort of auction:

OPENER	YOU	RESPONDER	PARTNER
1 ♡	Pass	2 ♡	Pass
Pass	*Double*		

why is the double for takeout? Could it not mean that you were *trapping* over the opening bid, and now are doubling for penalties? No, because the opponents have found a fit. They have enough points for an opening bid and a response; they have found a good trump suit. Even if you have a strong hand with a substantial trump holding, you cannot be sure of setting them. It is almost never profitable to double the opponents at the one– or two-level *unless the hand is a misfit.* So when the opponents pass out at a low level *after a suit has been raised,* a reopening double is for takeout; it is a "balancing" double to enable your side to compete for the part score.

Quiz

On this auction:

OPENER	PARTNER	RESPONDER	YOU
1 ♣	Pass	1 ♡	Pass
2 ♡	Pass	Pass	?

What would you bid with these example hands?

(a) ♠ A J x x x   ♡ x x   ◊ Q x x x   ♣ x x

(b) ♠ J x x   ♡ K Q x   ◊ A Q x x   ♣ 10 x x

(c) ♠ x x   ♡ x   ◊ K Q x x x   ♣ K Q x x x

(d) ♠ K x   ♡ Q x x x   ◊ 10 x x x   ♣ Q x x

(a) ♠ A J x x x   ♡ x x   ◇ Q x x x   ♣ x x

Bid two spades. Don't sell the hand without a fight. The opponents have found a fit, so you have one too. They have stopped short despite their fit, so partner must have enough points to make your bid safe.

(b) ♠ J x x   ♡ K Q x   ◇ A Q x x   ♣ 10 x x

Double. The same reasoning as above applies here, except that now *you* have the points and partner has the suit. Your reopening double is, in effect, a balancing over-call in partner's best suit.

(c) ♠ x x   ♡ x   ◇ K Q x x x   ♣ K Q x x x

Bid two notrump. This is the unusual notrump (for if you had a strong balanced hand, you would not have passed at your first turn) used in the balancing position; partner must take out in one of the minor suits. You could instead reopen with a three-diamond bid, but the unusual notrump gives you an extra chance—the opening might have been in a short club suit.

(d) ♠ K x   ♡ 10 x x x   ◇ Q x x x   ♣ Q x x

Pass. It should always be tempting to reopen when the opponents find a fit and stop short, but it is not mandatory. If you have a long suit, you may assume that partner has the points you need; if you have 10 points or more, you may assume that partner has the suit you need. But when you have neither, you must *not* assume that partner has both. If he had, he would have acted *directly* over one club or two hearts, instead of waiting for you to balance.

RESPONDING TO BALANCING BIDS

When your partner passes at his first turn and enters the auction only after the opponents find a fit and stop at a low contract, he is not looking for a game contract. His principal objective is to push the enemy to the three-level where they may be defeated; secondarily, he may hope to fulfill a low part-score contract of his own. So do not get excited when partner balances; do not raise his overcall or jump in response to his double. Partner based his action not on his own values alone, but also on what he can count on you to have. Nine times out of ten, he has already bid every point in your hand.

Responding to Balancing Overcalls

When partner balances with an overcall, *pass* even when you have a good fit and quite a lot of points. On this auction:

OPENER	YOU	RESPONDER	PARTNER
1 ◇	Pass	1 ♠	Pass
2 ♠	Pass	Pass	3 ♡
Pass	?		

pass with each of these hands:

♠ x x	♡ K J x x	◇ A Q x x	♣ x x x
♠ A x x	♡ K x x	◇ A x x x	♣ Q x x
♠ x	♡ Q J x x x	◇ Q x x	♣ Q J x x

Do not say to yourself, "If partner can bid three hearts without hearing from me, then I can raise him to four." The opponents' auction told him of your strength just as surely as if you had bid; in each example, your hand is what partner hoped you had—enough to give him a play for his contract. If partner had game ambitions, he would have overcalled directly over *one* spade.

What is more, if responder bids three spades after you pass three hearts on the auction above, you should pass again! Do not compete further or double the opponents with any of the example hands. Partner has succeeded in pushing the enemy one higher; try not to punish him for his daring. If you defeat three spades, the balancing overcall shows a profit, and if three spades makes, the reopening bid cost nothing. So you cannot lose and may well gain. Leave it at that.

Responding to Balancing Doubles

When partner balances with a double, respond at the cheapest level in your longest unbid suit, and then retire from the auction. Do not pass the double for penalties; do not jump in response; do not bid twice. On this sequence:

OPENER	PARTNER	RESPONDER	YOU
1 ◊	Pass	2 ◊	Pass
Pass	Double	Pass	?

if you hold:

♠ K Q x x　　♡ x x　　◊ K J x x　　♣ x x

bid two spades. Had partner doubled *one* diamond, you would have *jumped* to two spades, trying for game; but now game is not in view, since neither of you could bid directly. Note that you do not pass the double for penalties. The opponents can probably make that contract, for partner was not strong enough to double on the first round.

And if the opponents go to three diamonds over two spades, let them play it there. Do not bid three spades; do not double. Once again, partner has accomplished his objective—pushing the enemy one higher. If you defeat three diamonds, thank partner for getting them up high enough. He will not thank *you* for doubling even if they go down one—the strain on his heart will have been too great. If you continually put partner back in jeopardy by bidding again or doubling after his reopening bid has done its work, he will soon stop balancing with you. And then the enemy will steal far too many part-score hands.

WHEN *NOT* TO BALANCE

Misfit Auctions

Do not reopen the auction simply because the opponents have stopped at a low contract. They have given up on game for one of two reasons: because they do not have enough high cards, or because they do not have a fit. When they have found a fit but stay low, it is safe to compete— partner is marked with a respectable point-count and your side has a fit also; but when the opponents have a misfit it is often suicidal to reopen, for then you have no fit either and there is no presumption at all that your side has a fair share of the high cards. Consider this auction:

OPENER	PARTNER	RESPONDER	YOU
1 ♡	Pass	2 ♣	Pass
2 ♡	Pass	Pass	?

Suppose you hold the hand cited earlier as a typical balancing overcall:

♠ K J x x x   ♡ x x   ◇ K J x   ♣ x x x

Do not even consider reopening with two spades on this auction! Responder has announced a strong hand, and has passed under game only because he fears a misfit. The enemy hands could well be:

OPENER	RESPONDER
♠ Q 10 x	♠ A x x x
♡ A K J x x x	♡ x
◇ A x x	◇ x x x
♣ x	♣ A Q 10 x x

This leaves partner with:

♠ x   ♡ Q 10 x x   ◇ Q x x x   ♣ K J x x

You will be doubled and set from 3 to 5 tricks wherever you play the hand. Note that the opponents have a misfit, so that you have a misfit also. They stopped at a part-score with enough high-card strength to warrant a game bid *because they had a misfit;* therefore, it would be a disastrous error for you to assume that partner has a strong hand.

Here are two more examples of auctions in which the enemy have passed out at a low contract, but in which you should not reopen regardless of your hand:

OPENER	RESPONDER
1 ♡	1 ♠
2 ◇	Pass

and

1 ♣	1 ♡
2 ♣	2 ♡
Pass	

The key factor is that no suit has been supported. This means that you cannot assume that your side has either the fit or the points to make competition safe. So if you were not strong enough to bid directly, you are not strong enough to balance.

After One-Notrump Response

There is a type of auction in which the opponents clearly limit their hands even though no fit has been found. Both opponents have minimum values; it would be surprising to find them with more than 22 points in combined high cards.

OPENER	RESPONDER
1 ♡	1 NT
Pass	

or

1 ♡	1 NT
2 ♡	Pass

If you were in the pass-out position on either auction with a hand like:

♠ K x ♡ x x ♢ Q J 10 x x x ♣ Q x x

you could safely overcall in diamonds. Partner is marked with enough points to provide safety. But if you were sitting in the balancing position on either auction with some hand such as:

♠ K x x ♡ A x x x ♢ K x x ♣ J x x

you must pass, not reopen with a double! Since the opponents have not found a fit, there is no presumption that you have a playable trump suit. It is safe to reopen only when you require points from partner, not fit.

When you *do* reopen with a double on an auction in which the opponents have not supported a suit, for example:

OPENER	YOU	RESPONDER	PARTNER
1 ♠	Pass	1 NT	Pass
Pass	*Double*		

this double is for penalties. It means that you were trapping. You are not bidding values in partner's hand; you, yourself, have the best hand at the table. A second- or third-round reopening double is for takeout *only when the opponents have found a fit*. Then, you could not possibly want to double for penalties; but otherwise, you could not possibly feel safe in doubling for takeout.

6

OVER PREEMPTIVE OPENINGS

♠ ♡ ◇ ♣

Occasionally, your opponents will open the auction with
high bids—three-bids or four-bids—in an effort to shut
you out. When you have a lot of strength, this is frustrat-
ing. You know that the hand belongs to your side, but you
have very little room in which to find your best contract.
If you stab, you are likely to guess wrong and wind up
losing points even with most of the high cards. Yet if you
stay out of the auction, the opponents have picked your
pocket. Infuriating!

It is important to realize that there is no sure-fire defense against preemptive openings. There is no fancy
gadget which will allow you to bid as accurately in one
round of bidding as in four; the best bidders in the world
will sometimes be crowded into poor contracts by preempts and will have hands stolen from them once in a
while. That is why preemptive bids continue to be made.

You must accept the fact that you are unlikely to reach

a perfect contract after a preemptive opening! Concentrate on getting any reasonable return for your high cards. And, above all, be willing to be shut out by a shut-out bid —your opponent's weakness does not make you any stronger. A bridge player who cannot bear to let the enemy steal a hand from him is like a poker player who is never bluffed—a sure loser.

PASSING OVER PREEMPTS

This means that if you do not have the values to enter the auction at a high level, you pass. Over a one-spade opening bid, this hand:

♠ x x   ♡ A Q x x   ◇ K J x x   ♣ K x x

is a sound takeout double. Over a *three*-spade opening bid, it is not. You can afford to force partner to bid a suit at the two-level, but you cannot make him bid at the four-level. It is true that you could conceivably miss a game by passing, but if you double with hands of this strength you will have three disasters for every one makable contract you reach. Common sense indicates that the higher the level at which you plunge into the auction, the more strength you must have.

TAKEOUT DOUBLE OVER PREEMPTS

Point Count Requirements

The point-count requirements set up for takeout doubles in Chapter 2 allow for this—11 points is the minimum if partner can respond at the one-level, and 2 points extra is required for each additional level. Applied to the takeout double directly over a preemptive bid, this means that you need at least 15 points to double a three-club, diamond or heart opening, at least 17 points to double any preemptive opening from three spades to four hearts.

Another way to look at it is to assume that partner has about 8 points (this is his fair share of the remaining cards) and will respond in an unbid major suit. Thus, if you double a three-spade opening bid, you will be in a four-heart contract opposite 8 points, and you had better have at least 17 points yourself. If you double a three-heart opening bid, you will be in a three-spade contract opposite 8 points, and need 15 points yourself to be reasonably safe. Never double with a hand under the minimum requirements—even when you have your values you are taking a calculated risk, since you will go down if partner has a really bad hand; the risk becomes prohibitive when you have less.

Distributional Requirements for Double

The distributional requirements for the double of a preemptive opening are in one way more rigid than for the double of a one-bid. *The double of a major suit preempt promises at least four-card support for the other major.*

Suppose the bidding is opened with three spades on your right and you hold:

♠ x   ♡ J x x   ◇ A J x   ♣ A K J x x x

You should overcall four clubs instead of doubling. It would be reasonable to double a *one*-spade opening, for you can stand a two-heart response, but you dare not force partner to bid hearts at the four-level.

Any takeout double begs for a major-suit response. If partner answers in a four-card major suit when you have only three-card support, you are not likely to be in trouble at the one– or two-level; but at the three– or four-level, you can be headed for disaster. This is particularly true since a preemptive opening warns of a bad trump split. So be sure that you really want to hear the most likely response when you double a high bid for takeout; there is no room at the four-level to probe for a better trump suit if you cannot support partner's reply.

In contrast, you must take greater liberties with your *minor* suit holdings when you double a shut-out bid. If your right-hand opponent opens three spades and you hold:

♠ x x   ♡ K Q x x   ◇ K x   ♣ A K J x x

you should double, begging partner to bid hearts. Were the opening bid *one* spade, you would overcall in clubs. Partner will not pass if you have game, and you can show hearts secondarily if he bids—you have plenty of room, and there is no need to promise diamond support which you cannot deliver. But the preemptive opening leaves you no opportunity for such delicacy. You must keep your eye on the main chance—the major-suit game. And if partner responds in diamonds, you will have to pass, accepting what may be a poor contract. You cannot hope for complete accuracy against opponents' preempts; all you can do is proceed in the right general direction.

Quiz

What would you do over your right-hand opponent's preemptive bid in these situations?

(a) The opening is three diamonds. You hold:

♠ K Q x x   ♡ Q J x x   ◇ A x x   ♣ x x

(b) The opening is three hearts. You hold:

♠ J x x x   ♡ x   ◇ A Q x x   ♣ A J 10 x

(c) The opening is three spades. You hold:

♠ K Q 10 x   ♡ x x   ◇ A K x x   ♣ K x x

(d) The opening is three spades. You hold:

♠ x x   ♡ A K x   ◇ A Q 10 x   ♣ A K x x

(a) *Pass.* It is not your club holding which stops you from doubling—you expect a major suit response. But your point-count is insufficient to force partner to respond at the three-level. As we will see later, if partner has enough strength to make three of a major opposite your hand, he will jump to four when you double. And if he is good enough to make *four,* he will bid himself even though you pass.

(b) *Double.* You have 15 points (adding 3 points for the singleton in the enemy suit) and four cards in the unbid major, so you can force a response at the three-level. This is the rock-bottom minimum for the action.

(c) *Pass.* It would be profitable to blast partner speechless with a vicious DOUBLE! and penalize your opponent for his gay opening bid, but this is unethical. A double in a normal tone of voice is odds-on to get you a four-heart response and a substantial minus score. If you pass, you are sure of a small plus score even if partner does not reopen; and, as we will see, you have not given up all chance for a big set.

(d) *Double.* This is a bad bid, since you have only three-card support in the unbid major. But there is no good bid available; you have no long suit in which to overcall, and it is more than flesh and blood can bear to pass 20 points. Your overwhelming strength may bring four hearts home even with only seven trumps. And, after all, there is no law against partner holding five hearts, or responding in a minor, or bidding notrump. What is more, since you are short in spades partner may be long, and decide to pass your double for penalties.

RESPONDING TO PARTNER'S DOUBLE
Penalty Pass

You may have heard that partner's double of a preemptive opening bid is an "optional" double, half for takeout and half for penalties. This is not literally so; the double of any opening suit bid from one club to four hearts, inclusive, is intended for takeout. But there is nevertheless a little truth in the idea that partner's double of a high opening is "optional," for it is very easy for you to pass and convert the takeout into a penalty double.

There are two reasons for this. First, the opponents are up higher, so that you need fewer tricks to defeat them. Second, partner needs greater strength to make a takeout double of a high opening bid, so that a smattering of cards in your hand will produce a set. Suppose you hold:

♠ x x   ♡ Q J 9 x   ◇ J x x   ♣ A x x x

If your left-hand opponent opens one heart and partner doubles, you should not even consider passing for penalties. You need seven tricks to defeat the contract, and if partner has a light double declarer may well make overtricks; when partner has a strong double, you will still not beat one heart enough to make up for what you could have made at your own contract.

But if the opening is *three* hearts and partner doubles for takeout, you should pass his double for penalties. Now you need only five tricks, and you will surely get more, for partner is not allowed to make a light double at the three-level. Now you will collect enough against *three* hearts doubled to compensate you for your own contract, even if partner has the 17 or 18 points you need to make game.

However, if you hold the hand above when partner doubles a three-*spade* opening bid, do not give a thought to passing—bid four hearts. Partner has made a takeout double; if you pass, *you* have made the penalty double. And, just as for any penalty double, you require *length and strength in trumps* for the penalty pass.

If partner doubles a three-club opening bid and you hold:

♠ x x x   ♡ x x x   ◊ K 10 x x   ♣ x x x

do not pass; bid three diamonds. The weaker you are, the more surely will the enemy make their doubled contract, so do not be afraid to bid—you should be afraid to pass. You could pass had partner doubled a three-*diamond* preempt, for you have trump tricks. And had the opening bid been *four* clubs, you might gamble out a penalty pass of partner's double. You should have a fighting chance to defeat this contract since you need only four tricks, and partner has promised a *very* strong hand by doubling at such a high level.

Simple and Jump Responses

Normally, you will respond to partner's double by taking out into a four-card or longer major suit if you have one, into a minor suit or into notrump if you haven't. If your minimum response would not be a game bid (for example, if partner doubles a three-heart opening and you answer three spades) you may decide to *jump* in your suit. This, of course, requires extra values.

Remember that partner is already playing you to have 8 points in your hand. When partner doubles a one-bid, he must allow for you to have very little, since he and opener are likely to hold most of the high cards in the deck between them, but when the opening is a preempt— occasionally as much as 8 or 9 points in high cards, usually less—there are a lot of points missing. If you have 8 points, that is probably a little less than half of the missing strength, and nothing to get excited about. So if partner doubles a three-heart opening bid and you hold:

♠ Q J x x   ♡ Q x   ◊ K x x x x   ♣ x x

respond only three spades even though you could have a lot less. Your hand is worth 8 points—you discount the valueless heart queen and doubleton, but add 1 point each for the doubleton club and fifth diamond.

If the whole deal is:

```
                         RESPONDER
                      ♠ 10 x x x
                      ♡ x x
                      ◇ A Q 10 x
                      ♣ K x x
   PARTNER                                      YOU
♠ A K x x                                    ♠ Q J x x
♡ A x                                        ♡ Q x
◇ J x                                        ◇ K x x x x
♣ A 10 x x x                                 ♣ x x

                         OPENER
                      ♠ x
                      ♡ K J 10 x x x x
                      ◇ x x
                      ♣ Q J x
```

the bidding should go:

OPENER	PARTNER	RESPONDER	YOU
3 ♡	Double	Pass	3 ♠
Pass	4 ♠	All Pass	

Observe that partner raises to game (he would have passed had you responded four diamonds), for if you have the 8 points he expects, there will be a good play. Actually, you have to be both skillful and lucky to make the contract, for you hold a poorer hand than he hoped for. And what if you had held a worthless hand—if responder had your spade queen and diamond king? Then you would have been doubled in four spades and set 2 or 3 tricks. You must expect a bad result now and again when the opponents preempt; do not bawl partner out for overbidding—apologize to him for underholding. Enemy shutout bids force your side to guess, and partner was right to go along with the probability that you had the fair hand you were entitled to hold on the auction.

When you have a better hand than partner expects— 10 points or more, or very powerful distribution—you can think of jumping in response to the double. If partner doubles a three-club opening bid and you hold either of these hands:

♠ A x ♡ K J x x ◇ Q x x x ♣ x x x
♠ x ♡ Q 10 x x x x ◇ K x x x ♣ x x

jump to four hearts. If you were to respond three hearts instead, you would miss game when partner has a 15 or 16 point double. He would pass, playing you to have 8 points, not 10. (Had partner doubled a three-*spade* opening, you would, of course, bid four, not five, hearts with either hand; you jump only to make sure of reaching game.)

Cue-Bid Responses

Another frequent route to game after partner doubles a preemptive opening is the cue-bid of the enemy suit:

OPENER	PARTNER	RESPONDER	YOU
3 ♣	Double	Pass	4 ♣

This asks partner to bid his best suit and, like any cue-bid response to a takeout double, says nothing about your holding in the opponent's suit. You should employ the auction above with either of these hands:

(a) ♠ K Q x x ♡ A 10 x x ◇ x x ♣ x x x
(b) ♠ Q J x x ♡ A x ◇ A Q x x x ♣ x x

With hand (a), you are making sure of reaching the better major-suit game; rather than guess the right suit in which to jump to four, you pass the decision back to partner.

With hand (b), you are too strong to jump to four spades directly, so you cue-bid first to suggest slam (your cue-bid becomes a slam-try only when you bid over doubler's major suit response to it). Any hand of 13 points or more has slam possibilities when partner doubles at a high level, and slam investigation is best started with the cue-bid. But be wary of slam contracts when an opponent has preempted; your suits are not likely to split favorably, and you should often allow the enemy to talk you out of a slam which you would otherwise have stretched for. Bid a slam if you clearly have the values for it, but resolve any doubtful decision in favor of passing at game.

Quiz

Your left-hand opponent opens three clubs and partner doubles. What should be your action with these hands:

(a) ♠ x x x ♡ x x ◊ Q 10 x x x x ♣ A Q

(b) ♠ x x ♡ J x x x ◊ Q 10 x x ♣ x x x

(c) ♠ x x ♡ J x x x ◊ A Q 10 x x ♣ x x

(d) ♠ Q x x x ♡ x x ◊ A K x x x ♣ x x

(e) ♠ x x ♡ x x ◊ A x x x x ♣ K J x x

(a) ♠ x x x ♡ x x ◊ Q 10 x x x x ♣ A Q

Bid three notrump. With two club stoppers, you need only a little help from partner in diamonds to bring home this game contract. Do not worry about stoppers in the major suits—partner must have length and strength there for his double. Do not pass the double for penalties; you need length in trumps, as well as strength, for this action.

(b) ♠ x x ♡ J x x x ◊ Q 10 x x ♣ x x x

Bid three diamonds. You have been cheated of your fair share of high cards here, and are likely to be in trouble since partner will expect you to have more. So respond in the minor suit, not in the major; partner is much less likely to raise you, for he will see no game contract in prospect. You must not pass partner's double with such a weak hand; there is little chance of defeating three clubs.

(c) ♠ x x   ♡ J x x x   ◊ A Q 10 x x   ♣ x x

Bid three hearts. Now you have the strength partner will play you for, so go out of your way to respond in the major suit. If partner has four-card length in hearts and 17 points or more, he will raise you to a reasonable game contract.

(d) ♠ Q x x x   ♡ x x   ◊ A K x x x   ♣ x x

Bid four spades, since you have a better hand than partner can expect should you respond only three spades. Partner has not guaranteed four-card support (as he would, had he doubled three *hearts*); he may have four hearts and only three spades. But he *probably* has at least four spades, and when the opponents crowd the auction with a preempt you must often deal in probabilities instead of certainties. Your combined hands have enough strength for game, and four spades is likely to be your best game contract; so bid it. If it turns out wrong, graciously congratulate your opponent on the effectiveness of his bid.

(e) ♠ x x   ♡ x x   ◊ A x x x x   ♣ K J x x

Pass for penalties. You can expect a handsome profit, for you have length and strength in trumps, a fair hand, and shortness in partner's major suits (so that his high cards will take tricks on defense). It is conceivable that you could score more points playing the hand yourself in notrump or diamonds, but there is no way to find out whether this is so. Do not expect a maximum result every time the opponents preempt. Settle for a reasonable plus score.

OVERCALLING OVER PREEMPTS

Requirements

It requires just as much strength to overcall an opponent's preemptive opening as it does to double it. The difference lies in your distributional pattern. If you have good support for unbid major suits and a strong hand, it is more desirable to double; if you have a strong hand without the pattern for a double, or with a very good suit of your own, it is more desirable to overcall.

However, you must have a hand strong enough to provide safety at the level at which you are forced to bid. You could overcall a one-club opening with one heart holding:

♠ x x   ♡ A Q 10 x x   ◇ A J x x   ♣ x x

But you dare not bid *three* hearts over a three-club pre-empt. You are entitled to assume that partner has about 8 points and a doubleton heart. If that is all he has, you are in trouble at three hearts; if he has more, he will raise you and you will go down at a higher contract. With the example hand above, you must pass.

You need the same 15 points to *overcall* at the three-level (or 17 points at the four-level) that you have to have in order to *double;* only your distribution is different.

Examples

These are all reasonable overcalls after a three-club opening bid:

(a) ♠ A K J x x x   ♡ J x x   ◇ K Q   ♣ x x
(b) ♠ x x   ♡ K Q J x x   ◇ A Q x x   ♣ K x
(c) ♠ K x   ♡ A Q x   ◇ A J 10 x x x   ♣ x x

Example (a) would qualify for a takeout double, but the strong suit suggests an overcall instead. Examples (b) and (c) have distribution which prohibits a takeout double —a major suit for which there is no support.

In response to these overcalls, partner will pass when he has only the 8 points that you expect, and will raise to game with more. In the case of a minor-suit overcall, like example (c), he will try three notrump with a club stopper and a fair hand, or show a strong major suit if he has one.

Jumps to Game

When your hand can make game facing 8 points from partner, you must not overcall at the three-level; for then you might miss game. Jump right to game yourself over a three-club opening with either of these hands:

♠ A K Q x x x   ♥ x x   ♦ A Q J x   ♣ x

♠ x x   ♥ K Q J 9 x x   ♦ A J x   ♣ A Q

There is no assurance that partner will put down enough cards to let you make game, but he probably will. And you have to settle for probabilities when the opponents preempt.

The three notrump overcall is another gambling action which an enemy shut-out bid may force you to take. If you have 17 points or more, with stoppers in the opponent's suit and no other convenient action, bid three notrump. This should be your bid over a three-heart opening with these examples:

(a) ♠ x x   ♥ A Q x   ♦ K J 10 x   ♣ A K x x

(b) ♠ K x x   ♥ A x   ♦ A Q J x x x   ♣ Q x

You cannot double with either hand because you lack the required spade support, yet game is probable if partner has his share of cards. So bid the most likely game. Often three notrump is a remarkably good spot after an enemy preempt, since the long suit is in a weak hand which may have no side entry. Partner, in deciding whether to try for slam over your three notrump overcall (or over any other of your game bids after a preemptive opening), must remember that you have already played him to have some cards; you do not expect to make your contract facing a bust. So he should think of slam only if he has a strong opening bid of his own.

Immediate Cue-Bid

When you *can* make slam facing 8 to 10 points in partner's hand, that is, when you have an original two-bid in your hand, you show your strength by cue-bidding the opponent's suit:

OPENER	YOU
3 ♡	4 ♡

Partner is expected to jump in response if he has a fair hand. And if you repeat your cue-bid over partner's response:

OPENER	YOU	RESPONDER	PARTNER
3 ♣	4 ♣	Pass	4 ♠
Pass	5 ♣		

you are showing a gigantic two-suiter in the remaining unbid suits. For the auction above, you might hold:

♠ x   ♡ A K J 10 x x   ◇ A Q J 10 x x   ♣ Void

Partner, of course, must now take a preference (or a *jump* preference if he has useful cards) between your suits.

BALANCING AFTER A PREEMPTIVE OPENING

The high requirements for doubles and overcalls *directly over* a preemptive opening bid put a special burden on fourth hand in auctions like:

OPENER	PARTNER	RESPONDER	YOU
3 ♡	Pass	Pass	?

In the pass-out position, it is safe to lower the requirements for action, for you now know that responder does not have a very powerful hand (although he certainly does not have to be weak when he passes opener's shut-out bid). And in this position, it is necessary to lower the requirements, for otherwise two 14-point hands facing each other would never get into the auction.

When a preemptive opening is passed around to you, it is reasonable to act under the assumption that partner has about 10 points. This means that you may reopen with 13 points, a minimum opening bid, if your distribution is suitable. Once again, the choice between doubling and overcalling is made according to your pattern, not your strength.

Balancing Double

Shortness in the enemy suit should suggest a takeout double. It means that you have more cards to support any suit partner bids in response. And it increases the chance that partner is long in their suit, and is itching to have you double so that he can pass for penalties. Because you should have a heavy predisposition to balance with a double when you are short in opener's suit, partner can afford to pass directly over a three-heart opening with a hand like:

♠ K x ♡ A J 10 x x ◊ A x ♣ Q J x x

You are sure to be short in hearts, and so partner can bide his time and await developments. When you have a decent hand, you will reopen with a double and partner can lick his chops and pass; when you are too weak to reopen, you will beat the opponents a few tricks undoubled, and could have made nothing yourselves.

EXAMPLES

If left-hand opponent opens three diamonds, and partner and responder both pass, reopen with a double holding:

♠ Q x x x ♡ K J x x ◊ x ♣ A J x x
♠ A Q 10 x x ♡ K x x ◊ x ♣ J x x x
♠ K 10 x x ♡ A Q x x ◊ x x ♣ K x x

Your hand is worth 13 points in each example—adding 3 points for a singleton diamond or 1 point for a doubleton. If partner passes for penalties, you can contribute to the defense; if he bids, you can support his suit.

Partner should not jump to game in response to your balancing double unless he has 12 points or more. He should remember that 10 points is his normal expectancy; if you have a strong double, you can raise a minimum response.

Balancing Overcall

Reopening overcalls and responses to them follow much the same rules. When you will be safe facing the 10 points you expect from partner, balance with an overcall on hands unsuitable for a double. For example, if a three-club opening is passed around to you, overcall with these holdings:

(a) ♠ J x   ♡ A Q 10 x x x   ◇ K J x   ♣ x x
(b) ♠ K x   ♡ Q x   ◇ A K 10 x x x   ♣ x x x
(c) ♠ K Q 10 x x x ♡ A 10 x x x ◇ x x ♣ Void

You may not double with examples (a) and (b) because of shortness in a major suit. You should not double with example (c) because partner will very likely pass for penalties, and this will be unsatisfactory opposite your freakish distribution.

In responding to your overcall, partner must realize that you have already bid quite a few of his cards. He should raise only if he has 12 or more points in support of your suit.

Quiz

On the auction:

OPENER	PARTNER	RESPONDER	YOU
3 ♡	Pass	Pass	?

What is your action with these example hands?

(a) ♠ A x x x   ♡ x   ◇ A Q 10 x x x   ♣ x x
(b) ♠ K x   ♡ A J x   ◇ Q x x   ♣ K Q 10 x x
(c) ♠ K J 10 x x x x ♡ x ◇ A x x ♣ A Q
(d) ♠ K x x x   ♡ A Q 10 x x   ◇ Q x   ♣ x x

(a) ♠ A x x x   ♡ x   ◇ A Q 10 x x x   ♣ x x

Double. If partner passes for penalties or bids spades, you will be delighted. And if he answers four clubs? Pass, and take your loss gracefully. You are not entitled to a magnificent result every time out.

(b) ♠ K x   ♡ A J x   ◇ Q x x   ♣ K Q 10 x x

Three notrump. You may not double with a doubleton spade, and a four-club overcall figures to bypass the best game contract. If partner has his fair share of the outstanding cards, you will have a sound play for three notrump.

(c) ♠ K J 10 x x x x   ♡ x   ◇ A x x   ♣ A Q

Four spades. You should reopen with *three* spades without one of your aces, expecting partner to pass if he has only 10 points. Here, you can make game if partner has what you expect him to have, so jump right to it. If you go down, it will be cold comfort to reflect that most of the time you will make the contract, but it's true none-the-less.

(d) ♠ K x x x   ♡ A Q 10 x x   ◇ Q x   ♣ x x

Pass. Partner is short in hearts, yet still could not act directly. Therefore, you have no game. Take your sure profit by letting declarer struggle with his contract. As in all balancing positions, you do not reopen when you are long in the enemy suit.

AGAINST HIGHER PREEMPTIVE OPENINGS

So far, we have treated opening three-bids almost exclusively. However, everything written so far applies equally well to opening bids of four clubs or four diamonds (subject, of course, to the increased minimum values necessitated by action at the four-level). Opening four-heart bids are treated in much the same fashion: doubles are for takeout, but are often left in for penalties because of the level, if partner cannot respond in spades. The difference between the defense against opening four bids in the minors and against opening four-heart bids comes from the fact that four hearts is a game contract. This changes the odds. If you bid four hearts over an enemy four-diamond opening bid, get doubled and go down two, you have sustained a loss; but if you bid four spades over a four-heart preempt, you may be taking a good sacrifice when you go down. So you have a lot more to gain by bidding when the opponents are in game. Holding:

♠ A K 10 x x x   ♡ x   ◇ x x   ♣ K 10 x x

you should pass over an opening four-diamond bid at your right. You simply do not have the values for an overcall at the four-level; that is, you do not expect to make four spades if partner has his share of cards. But you should certainly bid four spades over a four-heart opening! Now you are willing to go down, in order to stop an enemy game. Partner, of course, must always allow for a shaded sacrifice overcall when an opponent opens with a game bid.

Doubles and Overcalls of Higher Preempts

Preemptive openings of four spades, five clubs and five diamonds are treated differently. These are such high bids that doubles become primarily for penalties, not for take-out. Still, they should be predicated on high cards, not on trump tricks; therefore, partner can take out into a long suit if he has a freak hand. But you are not asking him to come crashing into the auction at the five-level otherwise.

Over four-spade openings, a special bid is available: the overcall of four notrump. This can have no natural meaning; if you thought you could take ten tricks at notrump, you would double four spades for penalties. Thus, the four-notrump overcall is used as a three-suit takeout bid; partner is forced to bid his longest unbid suit at the level of five. To bid four notrump over four spades, you might hold:

♠ Void ♡ K Q J x ◇ K J 10 x x ♣ A K x x

You cannot use this artificial takeout bid over a four-heart opening, for this would get above the most likely game contract—four spades. Therefore, the takeout double is employed. A four-notrump overcall over four *hearts* should be used as the "unusual notrump" for takeout into a minor suit. Obviously, you can have no interest in spades.

DEFENSE AGAINST WEAK TWO-BIDS

A great number of American tournament bridge enthusiasts, including a majority of top-ranking players, use their opening bids of two diamonds, two hearts, and two spades as preemptive bids, reserving the artificial opening of two clubs for all very strong hands. A typical "weak" two-heart opening looks like this:

♠ x x ♡ K Q J x x x ◇ K x x ♣ x x

It does not have the freakish pattern of a three-bid; usually the suit is of no greater than six-card length. And the weak two-bid has greater defensive strength than most preemptive openings—it is just under the strength of an opening one-bid.

Two Diamond, Two Heart Openings

Treat weak two-bids in diamonds and hearts much as if they were one-bids. Double for takeout with support for all unbid suits, with particular emphasis on major suits. Overcall with strong hands that do not have the pattern for a takeout double. Naturally, you must bear in mind the bidding level—13 points is the minimum for a double, since partner must respond at the two-level; and skimpy overcalls are better left unmade.

Partner should make an effort to raise your overcall if

he would have responded cheerfully to an opening bid. You can then go on to game with a maximum, or pass if all you have is a sound minimum.

If you double, partner makes a minimum response with 0 to 8 points, jumps to invite game with 9 to 11 points, cue-bids with 12 points or more. These responses are exactly like those to a double of a one-bid (but one level higher, of course).

Two Spade Openings

The weak two-spade opening should be treated in much the same fashion as a three-bid. The takeout double promises four-card support for hearts, but must be made even without support for one of the minor suits if the heart support is there. Fifteen points is the minimum for this action, for here again you can play partner to have only 8 points. When partner has more than 8 points, he must jump in response to show you his strength.

The overcall and responses to it are based on the same presumption. Bid at the three-level with a strong suit and at least 15 points. Partner will raise if he has more than the 8 points you expect. If you can make game facing 8 points, for example with:

♠ x x   ♡ A Q J x x x   ◊ K Q 10 x   ♣ A

jump right to game.

Two Notrump Overcall of Weak Two Bid

The two-notrump overcall of any weak two-bid is the same as a one-notrump overcall of a one-bid—16 to 18 points with solid stoppers in the enemy suit. It tends to deny support for unbid major suits, for otherwise you should prefer to double.

THE FISHBEIN CONVENTION

Many players have adopted an artificial device to deal with opponents' preemptive openings—the "Fishbein Con-

vention." If you use this convention, the suit (notrump is
not counted) just above the opening is used as a takeout
double; the double is used for penalties. Thus, if your
right-hand opponent opens three diamonds and you hold:

♠ A Q x x   ♡ K x x   ◇ x   ♣ A Q x x x

you bid *three hearts,* the next higher suit, for takeout.
Partner may not pass three hearts. He must raise to four,
if hearts is his suit. He may take out to three or four
spades, to four or five clubs, according to his strength and
distribution.

If, on the same auction, you hold:

♠ A x   ♡ K x   ◇ A J 9 x x   ♣ Q 10 x x

you double three diamonds for penalties; and partner
must brave your wrath if he bids.

Several variations of this convention are currently in
play. In one of them, notrump is used for takeout, suit
bids are natural, and the double is for penalties. In another, the cheaper *minor* suit is used for takeout, major
suit and notrump bids are natural, the double is for penalties. These are attempts to remedy one flaw in the Fishbein Convention—that you must give up a perfectly useful, natural overcall in order to play it.

My recommendation is that you use none of these artificial bids. They all suffer from the same basic error—one
player must make the decision for the whole partnership.
If your right-hand opponent opens three spades and you
hold some hand like:

♠ K x   ♡ A K x x   ◇ A J x x   ♣ Q x x

you have no idea whether to double for penalties or force
partner to take out; it depends on what sort of hand he
has. It is a comfort to be able to consult partner by using
a takeout double which he can convert into a business
double if he wishes. These in-between hands are common;
the extreme hands with which you know what to do are

rare. And even when you have a solid business double of an opening preempt, you do not automatically lose because you are using takeout doubles and must pass; quite often, partner reopens with a balancing double and you collect your penalty anyway.

Still, you might like to try out the convention for yourself. The variation in which the cheaper minor suit is used for takeout seems to me to be best. It's really not such a bad idea to use a penalty double against opponents who like to open with scrawny, frisky three-bids. And somehow it is against human nature to have to pass over a preempt when you know that you could tear the enemy contract limb from limb.

7

OVER ONE-NOTRUMP
OPENING BIDS

♠ ♡ ◇ ♣

It is not possible to treat opponents' opening one-notrump
bids in the same way that you do their one bids in a suit.
This is because there is no good distributional pattern
for a takeout double of a one-notrump opening. If you
hold:

♠ A x x x   ♡ x   ◇ K J x x   ♣ K x x x

it is very desirable to double a *one-heart* opening bid for
takeout. Partner is most unlikely to have length only in
hearts, once hearts is opener's longest suit, and you have
excellent support for whatever unbid suit partner chooses.
But you could not double a *one-notrump* opening for
takeout. Since there is no presumption that opener is long
in hearts, the odds are heavy that partner will respond in
this suit—and what will you do then?

Whenever you double for takeout, you must assume

that partner will respond in your shortest unbid suit, for, because there are a limited number of cards in the deck, shortness in your hand implies length in partner's. When the opening is one notrump, there are four unbid suits; you can be prepared for a response in *all* suits only with two types of hand:

   (a) ♠ A Q x   ♡ Q x x   ◇ K J x x   ♣ A J x
   (b) ♠ K Q J 10 x x   ♡ A x   ◇ A J x   ♣ x x

With the high-card strength and distributional pattern of example (a), you can tolerate any response at the two-level. But fair support for four suits means good support for none; even if partner has moderate strength, he will be struggling to make 8 tricks at any contract. And if he *has* 5 or 6 points, you could take 7 or 8 tricks on defense against one notrump doubled, to make a surer and more substantial profit on defense.

With a hand like example (b), you are willing to hear any response at the two-level because you are prepared to bid over it. Your long suit and great strength guarantee safety; if partner has a few high cards you will make two or three spades. But again, you should prefer to defend against one notrump doubled rather than play for a part score. You can defeat the contract unaided with your own hand, and a little strength in partner's will produce a 2- or 3-trick set.

So the only distributional patterns which are in any way satisfactory for a *takeout* double of a one-notrump opening are much better suited to a *penalty* double. In consequence, *there is no such thing as a takeout double of a one-notrump opening.* A double is for business.

How much strength must you have to double one no-trump? This depends on what the opening bid means. A few old-fashioned bidders and a handful of ultra-moderns (like some of the Italians) use a rock-crusher one notrump opening—up to 20 points. Obviously, you will never double this rare opening; you must pass unless you have a distributional freak. Most of your opponents use the standard "strong" notrump—16 to 18 points. And many players today are switching to the "weak" notrump opening which I, personally, prefer—12 to 14 points. The minimum count for the penalty double, as well as much of your defensive strategy, varies with the point range of your opponents' opening bid.

DEFENSE AGAINST THE 16 TO 18 POINT NOTRUMP

Penalty Double

The two example hands cited earlier in this chapter are typical doubles of a standard 16– to 18-point one notrump opening. The first one:

(a) ♠ A Q x ♡ Q x x ◇ K J x x ♣ A J x

is a balanced hand approximately equal in strength to opener's. Why can you double for penalties when you are no stronger than your opponent? Because your high cards lie behind his! You have the bulk of your side's honors, and opener has most of his side's; therefore, almost all of your finesses will succeed, while his will fail. This makes the penalty double a good gamble, for you will defeat the contract more often than not. Of course, if your partner has nothing and opener's partner has all the missing strength (this is only about 7 points), you will be in trouble; however, this possibility is compensated for by the large set that results when your partner has more than his share of what little is outstanding. You have no guarantee of success, but the odds are in your favor.

When you have fewer points than opener, though, the odds are against you. You will lose, in the long run, if you double a one-notrump opening with:

(c) ♠ K Q x   ♡ A x x   ◇ K Q x x   ♣ 10 x x

Opener has from 2 to 4 points more than you, and your positional advantage does not make up for this. Also, here there are some 10 points missing to be divided between the weak hands. Dummy now figures to hold a few high cards—perhaps an ace behind one of your king-queen combinations; so your position behind the strong hand is not so great an advantage. You *could* be spectacularly successful with this sort of double, for partner *might* hold almost all the missing strength. But it is a poor gamble; you should pass.

The second earlier example:

(b) ♠ K Q J 10 x x   ♡ A x   ◇ A J x   ♣ x x

is an even better double of a one-notrump opening. Here, your advantage is not so much that you are behind declarer as that you have the opening lead. Even when the opponents have more points than your side, you will be able to take seven tricks before they can bring their high cards into play. And one king in partner's hand could yield a 3-trick set.

The criterion for this sort of double is not points, but fast tricks and stoppers. You must have a long suit which is easily established, high cards in at least two other suits (unless your suit is solid) so that the enemy cannot take their tricks before you get yours, and the reasonable expectation of 7 tricks in your own hand.

Examples

Double one notrump with:

(a) ♠ x x   ♡ A Q J 9 x x x   ◇ A x   ♣ K x
(b) ♠ A x   ♡ A x x   ◇ Q J 10 9 x x   ♣ A x
(c) ♠ A K Q J x x   ♡ x x   ◇ A x x   ♣ x x

You have fewer points than opener, but since you are on lead you can establish your long suit in time to defeat the contract. Do *not* double with:

(d) ♠ K J 10 x x x x   ♡ A Q x   ◇ K x   ♣ x
(e) ♠ K Q J 10 x x   ♡ x x   ◇ x x   ♣ A K x

In either case, the opponents may take too many tricks before your suit runs. In hand (d), this can happen because your suit is not solid enough; in hand (e), you do not have the required stoppers in side suits.

Over Partner's Double

When partner doubles an opening bid of one notrump, you should almost always pass. Do not be depressed by a very puny holding—you are not expected to hold much, for opener and partner have most of the points in the deck between them. Even with a ghastly hand like:

♠ x x x   ♡ x x x   ◇ x x x   ♣ J x x x

you should leave in partner's penalty double. Partner may have a long suit or overwhelming strength and may defeat the contract with his own hand. More often, however, he will have a strong balanced hand and one notrump doubled will make. But what could you do about it then? Had you run to two clubs, you would almost surely have been doubled, for an even greater loss. *It is never proper to take out the penalty double of one notrump with a balanced hand.* (Of course, if responder redoubles you must not pass unless you have 4 or 5 points; the opponents will make more in one notrump *redoubled* than they could by doubling you at the two-level. So take out into your lowest-ranking suit.)

When you hold a weak *unbalanced* hand, such as:

♠ x   ♡ J x x x   ◇ J x x x x x   ♣ x x

take the double out; here, to two diamonds. If partner has doubled on points, you will have a fighting chance to make your contract; if he has doubled with a long suit, he will now bid it. In either case, you are safe at the two-level, and need not defend against a doubled contract which you suspect will be made.

When you hold a fairly strong unbalanced hand, like:

♠ x   ♡ Q x x x   ◊ K J x x x x   ♣ x x

you should pass the double cheerfully; you are going to score a huge set, for dummy is coming down with practically no high cards. However, if your long suit were a major and you were vulnerable against non-vulnerable opponents, you might decide to *jump* in your suit, looking for game.

The Overcall

You are not compelled to pass every time you do not meet the high requirements for the double of a one-notrump opening; you may occasionally overcall in a suit with much weaker hands. But think twice before you overcall, and then think once more.

The overcall of an enemy strong notrump opening is the most dangerous bid in bridge. You know that opener has considerable defensive strength, including values in your suit. And what is worse, opener's partner knows it too! Responder is aware of the entire combined defensive potential of his side, and so is in magnificent position to double you. For example, if you overcall two hearts, and he holds:

♠ A x x   ♡ 10 x x x   ◊ K x   ♣ x x x x

he can safely double. In effect, he is looking at 23 points (for opener has at least 16) and six trumps (for opener has at least two).

If your right-hand opponent opens one notrump, and you hold:

♠ x x   ♡ A Q J x x   ◊ A x x   ♣ Q x x

pass; do not overcall two hearts. If you overcall, you will be doubled perhaps one time in three and set from 2 to 4 tricks. And you will gain nothing much on the two hands in three when you are not doubled. If your partner is weak, the opponents will proceed to their normal contract when they do not choose to double you; if your partner is strong, you may make a part score; but then you would have set the one-notrump contract anyway, and have exchanged a sure profit for a doubtful one. There is almost no hope for game, with a 16– to 18-point hand against you. You cannot even expect to compete effectively for a part score with your 13 points since opener has so many more high cards than you have.

You *can* expect to compete effectively, and perhaps even make game, when your distribution is freakish enough to destroy the defensive value of opener's high cards. A hand like:

♠ K Q 10 x x x   ♡ x   ◊ K J x x x   ♣ x

is a fine two-spade overcall of a one-notrump opening. Opener has many more points than you have, but this is a disadvantage offset by your distribution. Now you may make two or three spades when the enemy could make a part-score in notrump or hearts; you may have a cheap sacrifice against an enemy game; you could even have a game yourself if partner has a good fit.

The key feature of a good overcall, then, is freakish distribution. It is desirable, obviously, to have a long, strong trump suit. But it is more important to hold singletons or voids which will draw opener's fangs. If his high cards will cash against your contract, you cannot show a sizeable profit from your overcall. But if your short suits neutralize enough of opener's strength, you can give the opponents a battle in the auction.

Quiz

What would your action be with these hands, after a one-notrump opening at your right?

(a) ♠ A x   ♡ x x x   ◊ K Q J x x x   ♣ x x
(b) ♠ x   ♡ Q J 10 x x x x   ◊ x x   ♣ K J x
(c) ♠ A K x x x   ♡ x x   ◊ Q J x x   ♣ A x
(d) ♠ x x   ♡ Void   ◊ A J x x x x   ♣ K J 10 x x

(a) ♠ A x   ♡ x x x   ◊ K Q J x x x   ♣ x x

Pass. Your suit is strong enough for an overcall, but your distribution is too flat. You should be delighted to have the opponents in notrump; do not warn them off with a futile overcall.

(b) ♠ x   ♡ Q J 10 x x x x   ◊ x x   ♣ K J x

Bid two hearts. With your 7 high-card points against opener's minimum of 16, you are David fighting Goliath, but distribution is your slingshot. The 20 missing points in spades and diamonds can take only 3 tricks.

(c) ♠ A K x x x   ♡ x x   ◊ Q J x x   ♣ A x

Pass. You have 14 points but points do not make an overcall; opener has more than you have and his cards will cash against your flat distribution. Never overcall with 5-3-3-2 or 5-4-2-2 pattern. If you just cannot bear to pass so strong a hand, then double. This is a poor gamble, but it *might* produce a big profit. To overcall is to take a big risk with virtually no chance for substantial gain.

(d) ♠ x x   ♡ Void   ◊ A J x x x x   ♣ K J 10 x x

Bid two notrump. This is, of course, the unusual notrump—an overcall in both minor suits at once. A two-diamond bid is acceptable despite the broken suit, for you have exciting distribution. But the unusual notrump overcall is preferable. At the cost of one bidding level, it doubles your chance of finding a fit.

After Partner's Overcall

When your partner overcalls after a one-notrump opening, you have only two possible actions available; either you raise his suit or pass. His overcall is not an invitation to bid some foolish suit of your own. If you have a singleton or void in partner's suit, do not "rescue"; the shorter you are, the more surely you should pass. This applies even when the overcall has been doubled by responder. If partner has a two-suiter, he will bail himself out; after all, he has heard the double too.

To raise partner, you must provide him with fast tricks, not with points. Queens and jacks in side suits have little value; partner needs aces, or at least kings. A singleton or void in a side suit is priceless; value a singleton as a full trick and a void as 2 tricks if you have three-card trump support. You may raise partner if you think you can provide 3 tricks.

However, remember that game prospects are remote against a strong notrump opening. Partner's overcall is almost always an attempt to fight for a part score, so do not get too enthusiastic.

If partner overcalls 1 NT with two spades and you hold:

(a) ♠ x x x   ♡ Q J x   ◇ K J x x   ♣ K Q x
(b) ♠ K x x   ♡ x x   ◇ A x x x x   ♣ x x x

you should pass.

Example (b) is closer to a raise, for it will provide more fast tricks, but game is not in view.

However, with example (b), you should sacrifice in spades against an enemy game contract.

On the same auction, you should raise to three spades with these hands:

(c) ♠ x x x   ♡ A K x   ◇ A x x   ♣ x x x x
(d) ♠ J x x x   ♡ A x x x x   ◇ x x x x   ♣ Void

You can provide 3 fast tricks in either example. With

hand (d), you should sacrifice against an enemy notrump or club game contract.

The Two-Club Takeout Over One Notrump

There is one type of distributional pattern which justifies action over a strong notrump opening even without great strength or freakish distribution: excellent support for both major suits. If your right-hand opponent opens one notrump and you hold either of these hands:

♠ A J x x   ♡ K Q x x x   ◊ Q x x   ♣ x
♠ K 10 x x x   ♡ Q J x x x   ◊ x   ♣ A x

you should feel like getting into the auction. You have broken suits and considerably fewer points than opener, but you may be able to compete effectively *because your suits are high ranking.* If you find partner with a few useful cards or with a good fit, you could well make a part score or push the enemy overboard, for they must go one level higher to outbid you in a minor suit. It will pay you, therefore, to cater to this distributional pattern by setting aside a special bid for it, the overcall of two clubs.

The two-club overcall of a one-notrump opening bid* should be used as an *artificial* bid; that is, it has nothing to do with clubs. (It is like using the "Stayman Convention" over an opponent's notrump opening instead of over partner's.) It promises at least four cards in both spades and hearts, and asks partner to take out into the major suit he prefers.

How many points do you need to bid a "Landy" two clubs over one notrump? This depends on your distribution. With two four-card major suits, you should have 13 points in high cards. But with greater length in spades and hearts, you may bid with fewer points. Count 2 points extra for each card over four in either major in order to

---

* Usually referred to as the "Landy Convention," after Alvin Landy who suggested it for use against weak notrump openings.

get up to the 13-point requirement. These examples are minimum two-club overcalls:

♠ A K 10 x   ♡ Q J 10 x   ◇ K x x   ♣ x x

♠ Q 10 x x x   ♡ A J 10 x   ◇ A x   ♣ x x

♠ K x x x x   ♡ A Q x x x   ◇ x x   ♣ x

♠ Q 10 x x x   ♡ K Q 10 x x x   ◇ Void   ♣ x x

All count to 13 points for the purpose of this takeout bid.

Responding to the Two-Club Takeout

When partner bids two clubs over an opposing notrump opening, your first duty is to choose between his two major suits. If you have a four-card or longer major, you bid it; and if you have not, you respond in a three-card spade or heart suit. In this respect, the two-club takeout is like the "unusual notrump"; partner is asking not for *your* longest suit, but for your *choice* between his suits.

Thus, with each of these examples:

(a) ♠ x x x   ♡ J x x x   ◇ x   ♣ Q J 10 x x

(b) ♠ x x   ♡ 10 x x x   ◇ K J x x x x   ♣ x

(c) ♠ x x   ♡ Q x x   ◇ A Q x x x   ♣ x x x

you should answer two hearts to partner's two-club takeout. Note that you do not pass two clubs with example (a), or bid diamonds with examples (b) and (c). You have a clear-cut preference for hearts over spades, and should show it.

It is not absolutely forbidden to pass two clubs, although this is unexpected and radical action. Still, if you hold great length in clubs, shortness in the majors, and a weak hand, for example:

♠ x x   ♡ x   ◇ J x x   ♣ Q J 10 x x x x

you should pass the takeout.

Likewise, a two-diamond response to two clubs is possible, although rare. It indicates length in diamonds and no preference for one major over the other. For example, respond two diamonds with:

♠ x x   ♡ x x   ◊ K J 10 x x x   ♣ K x x

However, remember that while you are *allowed* to pass the two-club takeout or answer two diamonds, you are *expected* to respond in a major suit.

It is possible to make a jump response in a major suit in order to invite game. Likewise, partner may raise your simple response if *he* has game ambitions. But both of these actions are very rare, for neither of you should expect to be able to make game against a 16- to 18-point opening bid. When game tries are made, they should be based on freakish distribution and fit, not on high cards. For example, suppose that partner bids two clubs over one notrump and you hold:

(a) ♠ A K x x x   ♡ Void   ◊ x x x x   ♣ x x x x
(b) ♠ Q J x x x   ♡ x x x   ◊ K J x   ♣ K x

With (a), jump to three spades. You have the perfect pattern in support of partner—length in one of his suits, shortness in the other. Your distribution is good enough to produce game if partner has an unbalanced pattern himself.

But with hand (b), bid only *two* spades. Your point-count is impressive, but game cannot be made on high-card points against a strong notrump opening. Your minor-suit kings are probably valueless, and your distribution is unexciting.

Similarly, if you yourself have bid two clubs over a one-notrump opening with one of these hands:

(c) ♠ K J 10 x x x   ♡ A J 10 x x   ◊ x   ♣ x
(d) ♠ A K x x   ♡ K Q x x x   ◊ K x   ♣ x x

and partner replies two spades, raise to three spades with (c), but pass with (d). Distributional values, not point-count, give you game possibilities.

In the "Balance" Position

All of the bids described so far—doubles, overcalls, or two-club bids—have been made in the *direct* position, right over the one-notrump opening. When the opening bid is, instead, on your left, and one notrump is passed around to you in fourth seat, do these bids change in meaning? No, but there are differences nonetheless.

The two-club takeout and the overcall can be used a little more freely, now that responder has passed the one-notrump opening. Responder *may* have as much as 7 points, but at least you are not sandwiched between two strong hands; and partner figures to have some high cards. These hands:

(a) ♠ J 10 9 x x x   ♡ x   ◇ Q J x x x   ♣ x

(b) ♠ Q 10 x x x   ♡ A x x x x   ◇ x x   ♣ x

would be too weak for action directly over a one-notrump opening. But in the pass-out position, you should overcall two spades with example (a), or bid two clubs with example (b). The usual "balancing" theory prevails: since the enemy have passed out at one notrump, partner must have the high cards to make your competition effective. All you need in the "balance" position is the distributional pattern; the fewer high cards you have, the more partner must have.

In contrast, the requirements for the penalty double cannot be similarly lowered in the reopening position. If you hold some hand such as:

♠ K Q x   ♡ A J x   ◇ Q J 9 x   ♣ J x x

you should pass either when one notrump is opened at your right, or when it is opened at your left and passed around to you. True, responder's pass makes it more likely that partner has some cards, but it is by no means certain. And this is offset by two new considerations. First, opener's strength lies *behind* yours, so that the cards are placed favorably for the enemy, poorly for you. Second, you are not on lead, so that partner will have to guess in the blind at which suit to attack first. In consequence, the penalty double must be used very sparingly in the "balance" position. If anything, the requirements are a little higher. Without a good suit to bid (or to jump in if you are very strong) you should have *more* points than opener—at least 17 or 18 points—in order to double. Pass any weaker balanced hand, and hope to defeat the contract. But don't be surprised if one notrump makes easily despite 15 or 16 points in your hand.

DEFENSE AGAINST THE 12- TO 14-POINT NOTRUMP

If your opponents are using the "weak" notrump opening, your defensive tools—the penalty double, the overcall, the "Landy" two-club takeout for majors—are the same. But your objectives are different, for now your side may well have a game (or even a slam) and there are prospects of a spectacular set when responder is weak. It pays to enter the auction much more freely. Of course, it is still dangerous to bid over one notrump, for although opener is rigidly limited, responder may be strong, and is in magnificent position to double you. But the potential gain from contesting the auction is much greater, for it is quite likely that your side "owns" the hand.

The Double

The double of a 12- to 14-point notrump opening is still for penalties. Just as over a strong notrump, the double is made with two different patterns: a strong balanced hand, or an unbalanced hand with a suit which will "run." Here are typical examples:

(a) ♠ K x ♡ Q J 10 x ◇ A K x x ♣ Q x x
(b) ♠ A x ♡ K x x ◇ K Q J x x x ♣ x x

Note that these hands are not strong enough to warrant a double of a 16– to 18-point notrump opening. But since opener is weaker, you need less in order to expect to defeat him. With hand (a), you are a favorite to set one notrump because you have more points than opener. With hand (b), your chief advantage is in having the opening lead; your high-card holding is only about the same as opener's but you will get your tricks first.

Example (b), with its long, easy-to-establish suit, is the preferable hand pattern for a penalty double of a weak notrump opening. The double with a strong balanced hand often fails to show a profit. Doubler does not have the positional advantage that he has over a strong no-trump, for dummy figures to show up with a few high cards now that opener is weaker.

An auction that goes:

OPENER	YOU	RESPONDER	PARTNER
1 NT	Double	Pass	Pass
Pass			

makes for a difficult time on defense. Declarer sees the full resources of his partnership, and knows just which suits to attack. You are in the dark, and must guess. This guess-work begins with the opening lead; when you have no long suit to attack, your lead may well get the defense off to a false start from which it will never recover.

Therefore, having a good opening lead is a key consideration in deciding whether to double a weak notrump opening. Example (a) above has a safe but attacking lead, the heart queen, and thus is a perfectly suitable double.

But a hand like:

♠ K x x   ♡ J x x x   ◇ A Q x   ♣ A J x

is a poor double even though it contains more points than opener holds, for it has no good lead. Pass 13– to 15-point balanced hands that have this flaw, for your slight advantage in high cards is more than overbalanced by opener's advantage as declarer. Of course, when you hold 16 points or more, your weight of high cards forces you to double regardless. Still, you must expect an occasional poor result.

After Partner Doubles

When partner doubles a weak notrump opening, you should pass with all balanced hands regardless of strength. This should represent your greatest chance for profit when your side has the majority of points; and it will likely be your smallest loss if they have more points than you.

However, you must not stand for one notrump doubled when you have wild distribution. For example, with these hands:

(a) ♠ x   ♡ J x x x x x   ◇ 10 9 x x   ♣ x x
(b) ♠ x   ♡ K J 10 x x x   ◇ K J x x   ♣ x x

you should take out. Bid two hearts with example (a); you probably cannot set one notrump, and should lose less playing the hand in your suit. Bid *three* hearts with example (b); you should set one notrump, but you may not set it enough to make up for your likely game at hearts. (Nonvulnerable against vulnerable opponents, you might gamble out a pass with example (b).)

After partner doubles a weak notrump opening, responder will often "run" to two of a suit. What do you do then? Double the rescue bid when you have a good trump holding, such as four-card length or a strong three-card suit. Bid a suit of your own if you had intended to take out the double had responder passed. Otherwise, pass around to partner. Suppose on this auction:

OPENER	PARTNER	RESPONDER	YOU
1 NT	Double	2 ◇	?

you hold one of these hands:

(a) ♠ A x x x   ♡ x x   ◇ J 10 x x   ♣ x x x
(b) ♠ K 10 x x x   ♡ K x x   ◇ x x   ♣ Q x x
(c) ♠ Q 10 9 x x x   ♡ x x   ◇ x   ♣ J x x x

With example (a), *double*. If partner has a balanced strong hand, he will pass, and the contract will be defeated handily; if he is unbalanced, he will not stand for your double, but will take out into his long suit.

With example (b), *pass*. If partner has diamond length of his own, he will double for penalties again, and you will pass. And if partner is unable to double, he will make a bid; now you can show your strength and your suit by acting at your second turn. You are assured this second chance to speak, for partner *may not double one notrump and then pass out the rescue*. His double commits him to bid again in this position.

With example (c), bid two spades. You were going to take out to two spades even if responder had passed, so you do it anyway. You are not interested in learning whether partner can double two diamonds; since you would not stand for this double, you take out in advance. (Add an ace to your hand and you would jump to three spades directly.)

If responder redoubles after partner doubles one notrump, do not pass with fewer than 5 points even if you have balanced distribution. Run to two of your lowest ranking suit. The chances are that you will be doubled and set, but this is cheaper than letting the enemy make their redoubled contract, possibly with overtricks.

The Overcall

Just as over a strong notrump opening, the principal requirement for an overcall is unbalanced distribution. No hand with a 5-3-3-2 pattern qualifies for an overcall, no matter what its strength. (It might well qualify for a *double* if it is powerful enough.) However, virtually any hand with 6-4-2-1 pattern should tempt you to overcall. If you hold:

♠ K 10 9 x x x ♡ x ◇ x x ♣ K Q x x

bid two spades over a weak notrump opening. The deal

may well belong to your side, and, even if it does not, your overcall will make the auction difficult for the opponents. The weak notrump opening is a semi-preemptive measure; when you overcall, you may turn this weapon of preemption against the enemy.

Quiz

One notrump (weak) is opened to your right. What is your action with these hands?

   (a) ♠ A K J x x   ♡ x x   ◇ J x x   ♣ K x x

   (b) ♠ A K J x x   ♡ A x x   ◇ J x   ♣ Q 10 x

   (c) ♠ A K J x x   ♡ x x   ◇ x   ♣ Q 10 x x x

With example (a), *pass.* Your distribution is too flat for an overcall, and your strength is such that you cannot make game unless partner can bid independently. If he does not bid, defending against one notrump figures to be your best chance for a profit.

With example (b), *double.* Again your pattern is wrong for an overcall, but now your hand is suitable for the penalty double: more strength than opener and a good opening lead.

With example (c), *overcall* two spades. Here you have fewer points than opener, but your distribution is exciting. And this is what makes for a good overcall against a notrump opening.

Response to Partner's Overcall

When partner overcalls a weak notrump opening, you should behave much as if the opening bid had been a "strong" notrump. That is, you pass with all mediocre hands. You raise partner's suit if you can provide about 3 fast tricks (and raise a major-suit overcall to game if you can provide more).

Now, though, it is possible for you to hold enough strength (14 to 16 points) to make game on power even with no fit for partner's suit. With such a hand, bid two notrump. Partner should show a second suit or rebid his first suit if he has a minimum, strictly distributional overcall. With greater strength, he can jump in his first or in a second suit, or raise to game in notrump. When partner overcalls, remember that he cannot hold a strong suit along with the high-card values of a sound opening bid, or he would double instead. Therefore, proceed with caution.

The Two-Club Takeout

The requirements for a "Landy" two-club bid over a weak notrump are virtually identical with those over a strong notrump opening. That is, you promise four cards in each major and 13 points; for each additional major-suit card, you can lower the minimum by 2 points. Actually, you might have much *more* strength to bid two clubs over a *weak* notrump than over a strong one. Hands like:

♠ A K x x   ♡ K Q 10 x   ◇ K J x   ♣ J x
♠ A 10 x x x   ♡ K Q x x   ◇ A J   ♣ K x

would make satisfactory *doubles* of a strong notrump opening. In contrast, over a *weak* notrump it is better to bid two clubs. The difference is that your side is now much more likely to have a game. The penalty you exact from one notrump doubled may be insufficient to compensate for what you could have made yourself, particularly since you do not have a clearcut, good opening lead with either example. In addition, your "positional" advantage over the notrump bidder is less against a weak notrump opening for dummy will hold some honors behind yours, so the penalty is less sure.

Response to "Landy"

The fact that game may be scored frequently against a weak notrump opening affects your responses to partner's two-club takeout. If you hold a poor hand, you make a "negative" response of two of your longer major (a three-card suit if necessary), or bid two diamonds, or (rarely) pass with long clubs. But if you hold 9 points or more in support of either major (adding for distribution, but discounting secondary values of queens, jacks, doubletons, etc., in the minor suits where partner is short), you must make a positive response.

The most common positive response is a jump in a major suit. To bid:

OPENER	PARTNER	RESPONDER	YOU
1 NT	2 ♣	Pass	3 ♡
			(or 3 ♠)

you should have 9 to 11 points in support, with at least four cards in the major suit. For the auction above, you might hold:

♠ K x   ♡ K Q x x   ◊ J x x x x   ♣ x x

This hand counts to 9 points: 8 in high cards (not adding for the worthless ◊ J) plus 1 point for the doubleton spade (nothing for the doubleton *club*). Partner is expected to go on to game if he has extra values, but to pass if he holds a minimum. That is, if he has bid two clubs with:

♠ A Q x x   ♡ A J x x x   ◊ x x   ♣ x x

he should pass your jump response. However, he would raise to game if he held an extra control (a minor-suit king, for example) or with better pattern (two five-card major suits, for example). Since partner will pass your jump response when he has a minimum, you must leap all the way to game when you hold a four-card or longer major and 12 points or more.

What if you hold a game-going hand but lack four-card support for either of partner's major suits? Then, make the forcing response of two notrump. Over this, partner should bid his five-card suit; without one, he should bid his longer minor suit. Now you will be in position to select the final contract. For example, suppose you hold:

♠ A x x   ♡ K x x   ◊ A J 10 x   ♣ x x x

The auction goes:

OPENER	PARTNER	RESPONDER	YOU
1 NT	2 ♣	Pass	2 NT
Pass	?		?

If partner bids three of either major, you will raise to game. If he bids three clubs, you can bid three notrump. And if he bids three diamonds, your best bet is probably to pass; although your side has the strength for game, you have no suit to play in, and the clubs are too shaky for notrump.

There are two other positive responses to partner's Landy two-club bid. These are the rare bids of three clubs and three diamonds. They show a magnificent suit at least six cards long and enough points to make game likely. However, partner should pass if the hand is a misfit, if his values were largely in major-suit distribution instead of in high cards.

In the Balance Position

When you are in fourth seat and a weak notrump opening is passed around to you, your approach to doubles, overcalls and takeout bids must be quite different. What has changed? First, there is less prospect of a juicy set (if opener's partner had a ghastly hand, he would not have passed one notrump and waited patiently for the axe to fall, but would have run out to a suit). Second, and more important, you are *not on lead* when one notrump is passed around to you; thus, your defensive prospects are not so bright when you have a strong suit: partner will lead something else.

EXAMPLES

Suppose that you hold an example hand we saw earlier:

♠ A K J x x   ♡ x x   ◇ J x x   ♣ K x x

If one notrump is opened to your *right*, you should pass. However, if one notrump is opened to your *left* and passed to you, overcall two spades. If you do not, partner will get the defense off to a false start with his opening lead, and the enemy may make a part score on a hand that belongs to you. This is a serious loss, so the risk of bidding is outweighed by the risk of passing.

Similarly, another hand we saw earlier must be treated differently:

♠ A x   ♡ K x x   ◇ K Q J x x x   ♣ x x

This was a fine penalty double of one notrump *directly over* the opening, since you were on lead. But you must not double in fourth seat, since partner is unlikely to lead diamonds. Simply overcall two diamonds. (With a strong major suit in a hand of considerable power in the pass-out seat, make a *jump* overcall to invite game. The jump overcall is preemptive directly over one notrump, but is strong in the reopening position.)

The next example was a sound *direct* double of a weak notrump opening:

♠ K x   ♡ Q J 10 x   ◇ A K x x   ♣ Q x x

After one notrump–pass–pass, however, the double is not nearly so attractive. First, partner must make a blind lead and thus your chance of defeating the contract is less. Second, the fact that your right-hand opponent passed one notrump means that he holds a balanced hand of some merit; therefore, there is not much chance of a large penalty. To double risks a huge loss when your partner has little strength, and there is too little prospect of a huge profit to compensate. You should pass one notrump, and hope to defeat the contract.

Clearly, the penalty double has little utility in the pass-out position against a weak notrump opening. Therefore, this double:

OPENER	PARTNER	RESPONDER	YOU
1 NT	Pass	Pass	Double

should be for *takeout* into a major suit. It should be used on just those hands with which you would have bid two clubs, Landy, *directly over* one notrump. And partner should respond to your double almost exactly as if you had used Landy. He does, however, have the option of passing for penalties, and he should do so when he has length and strength in the minor suits and no fit for your majors.

Natural Two-Club Overcall

The overcall of two clubs in the reopening position is natural, promising clubs. As we have seen, it is very desirable to overcall in any long, strong suit in fourth seat. There is no need to deny yourself the opportunity of over-calling in clubs, since the double is used for takeout.

Finally, let me point out that there is another situation in which your bid of two clubs over *any* notrump opening is natural, showing club length, even though you and partner use the Landy Convention. This is when you are a passed hand. Obviously, you cannot be strong enough to double one notrump for penalties; thus, the double by a passed hand is for takeout into a major suit. So the two-club overcall is no longer needed as a takeout bid and means just what it says.

8

PENALTY DOUBLES

♠　♡　◇　♣

There are actually three different types of penalty doubles used in bridge. Probably the most common variety and surely the most profitable is the double of enemy contracts when the hand belongs to your side. (Partner opens the bidding and an opponent enters the auction when you are strong; the opponents take a sacrifice against your game contract; etc.) This sort of penalty double has little to do with defensive bidding; you merely decide that you can score more points by setting the opponents than by bidding further yourself. But the other two types of penalty double are truly defensive, not offensive weapons: (1) the double of a high enemy contract which you expect to defeat, even though the hand clearly belongs to them, not to you; (2) the double which tells partner which suit to lead.

The opponents bid merrily along and reach their final contract; you have been passing throughout with a fairly good hand, and suspect that they have overbid. It is tempting to say double, but should you?

The first consideration is this: is the final contract a partial, a game, or a slam?

DOUBLING PART SCORES

If it is a part-score, *do not double.* (This applies to hands which belong to the opponents, not to hands in which your side has more than half the points.)

Suppose you hold:

♠ A J 10 x   ♡ x x   ♢ A Q x x   ♣ K J x

The bidding is opened at your left with one spade and proceeds:

OPENER	PARTNER	RESPONDER	YOU
1 ♠	Pass	1 NT	Pass
2 ♡	Pass	2 ♠	Pass
3 ♠	Pass	Pass	?

Despite your strength, you could not enter the auction earlier; you had no suit in which to overcall, and dared not double one notrump for takeout without heart support. Your best bet was to trap-pass, and hope the enemy got too high. Should you now spring your trap and double?

You do expect to defeat the contract, but you must not double it! Suppose you set three spades one trick doubled. You will score 100 instead of 50 points; the double gains 50 points. If you set the contract 2 tricks (and this is the most you can expect, for opener has at least 16 points and responder has 6 or 7), you will score 300 instead of 100; the double gains 200 points. Let us say that the double will net an average of 100 points when you defeat three spades.

But what if the contract makes? Then you lose 180 instead of 90, plus the 50 point bonus for fulfilling a doubled contract. Worse, the opponents now score a game and a non-vulnerable game is worth approximately 250 points more than a part-score. So the net loss from the double comes to 400 points.

When you double, then, you give away odds of four to one. Even if you set the opponents three times out of four, you will have lost points, so how can it be right to double? And this would apply equally if the opponents were vulnerable. The profit from the double would be greater when you set the contract. But the potential loss is greater too, for the game which you present the enemy when they make their contract is much more valuable when they are vulnerable.

Just about the only exception to the rule against doubling part-scores comes when the opponents clearly advertise a misfit:

OPENER	RESPONDER
1 ◇	1 ♠
2 ♣	2 ♡
3 ♣	3 ♡
4 ♣	

When you double bidding like this, you are still laying odds of four to one. But if you have trump length and strength, the contract will not make one time in ten, so you will gain handsomely in the long run.

Remember that the "don't double partials" principle has nothing whatever to do with an auction like:

PARTNER	OPPONENT	YOU
1 ♠	2 ♡	Double

When you double here with a hand such as:

♠ x   ♡ K J 9 x   ◇ A Q x x x   ♣ J x x

you are *not* giving four to one odds. You expect to gain a lot more than one or two hundred points by the double; the contract may go down 700 or 900, for the opponents have at most 15 or 16 points in their combined hands, not

23 or 24. And you would cheerfully give *ten* to one odds that you will defeat two hearts if partner stands for your double.

DOUBLING GAMES

The double of a *game* contract is considerably more advantageous, mathematically speaking. Consider our earlier example:

♠ A J 10 x   ♡ x x   ◊ A Q x x   ♣ K J x

If the auction goes:

OPENER	PARTNER	RESPONDER	YOU
1 ♠	Pass	1 NT	Pass
2 ♡	Pass	2 ♠	Pass
3 ♠	Pass	4 ♠	?

a double has a better gain/loss ratio. You are still unlikely to set the contract more than 1 or 2 tricks, for now responder has extra strength (which partner would have, had responder passed).

So the average *gain* from doubling will again be about 100 points, or 200 if the opponents are vulnerable, when you defeat the contract.

The *loss*, if four spades doubled makes, will be 120 points plus the 50-point bonus, or 170 points in all.

Thus, the double risks 170 points to gain 100 or 200 points, not such fearful odds.

However, two other factors weigh against a double. First, the double may disclose to the opponents the location of your cards, enabling them to make a contract they might otherwise have lost, or letting them save a trick even when they go down. Second, the opponents may have the impertinence to redouble when their favorable distribution will permit them to make the game; and then the double will lose heavily. All in all, you must defeat at least two out of every three game contracts you double in order to show a net profit.

Should you double with the example hand? Yes, indeed. The opponents have struggled up to game after each limited his hand severely: responder by answering one notrump originally and by rebidding two spades, opener by failing to jump to three hearts at his second turn or to four spades at his third. This doesn't mean that the contract must go down, but it does indicate that the enemy have stretched their values and need good breaks to make game. They are getting bad breaks, for the trumps do not split, and whatever heart strength is missing lies behind declarer. And when the opponents need good luck and are getting bad luck, you should double them. Another attractive feature of these "stretched" auctions is that neither opponent can have enough extra strength to warrant a redouble, even if the contract can, by some chance, be made. But had the bidding gone:

OPENER	RESPONDER
1 ♠	1 NT
3 ♠	4 ♠

you should not dream of doubling. The opponents are still getting bad breaks, but now they may be able to afford them since either one may have undisclosed extra strength. And that opponent may well redouble if you double a "jumpy" auction like this.

Doubling by Ear

A key consideration in deciding whether to double, then, is the sound of the opponents' bidding. Auctions like:

OPENER	RESPONDER
1 ♡	2 ♡
3 ♡	4 ♡

or

OPENER	RESPONDER
1 ◇	1 NT
2 NT	3 NT

are tempting to double, for each opponent has strained to reach game. But auctions like:

OPENER	RESPONDER
1 ♡	2 ♣
3 ♡	4 ♡

or

OPENER	RESPONDER
1 ◊	2 NT
3 NT	

must almost never be doubled. Either opponent may have strength in reserve—not sufficient for slam, perhaps, but enough to redouble, confident of making game even against an unlucky lie of cards.

Obviously, you do not double the opponents simply because they have stretched to reach game. They expect to make their contract, and will do so more than half the time. The limited auctions tell you not that the enemy will go down, but that they are on thin ice, that they cannot survive adverse distribution of key suits or high cards. Usually, you can look at your own hand and tell whether the opponents are running into good luck or bad. And when the lie of cards is foul for them and fair for you, double any game contract that the opponents have struggled to reach.

This decidedly does *not* mean to double a limited game auction whenever you hold a strong hand. Suppose the bidding goes:

OPENER	PARTNER	RESPONDER	YOU
1 ♠	Pass	2 ♡	Pass
2 ♠	Pass	3 ♡	Pass
4 ♡	Pass	Pass	?

Should you double if you hold:

♠ A x x   ♡ A x x   ◊ A Q x   ♣ J x x x

Certainly not! This is the sort of auction that you should like to double, but only when the opponents are running into hard luck. And here they figure to have good luck, for trumps split favorably, and if declarer needs a finesse against partner for the queen or jack, it will work; spades split, and if declarer needs the ace of spades on side, it is; the diamond king is likely to come down behind you in the dummy. You have a magnificent hand, but this is not bad luck for the enemy. They knew they didn't have your cards when they bid; what has happened is that all the missing honors are concentrated in your hand. This is a *good* break for them, for it impedes the defense. You would have a much better chance to defeat four hearts if you had an ace fewer (then partner could get in and lead to your diamond tenace).

On the same auction, you *should* double if you hold:

♠ x   ♡ Q 10 9 x   ◇ A x x   ♣ Q J 10 x x

You have much less in high cards, but this only means that partner is stronger. Here the opponents are in trouble. Trumps do not split and the finesse is wrong for them; spades do not split, and any finesse they need in that suit will fail. They will lose at least 2 more tricks than they might with better breaks; and on their auction, they cannot afford to lose extra tricks. This, then, is when you double an enemy game contract: with both opponents limited, you know that they need good luck to bring their game home; and you can see that their suits split unfavorably and that their finesses will lose.

Doubling Slams

This sort of speculative double of a high enemy contract should almost never be made when the opponents reach a *slam*. Slam auctions are never the "strained" sequences that tempt you to double; if both opponents were limited, they would have stopped at a game. Anyone will occasionally stretch his values in order to bid a "thin" game contract; but no one bids a slam without the solid expectation of making it. Therefore, bad breaks may not be enough to defeat a slam, particularly when declarer is warned by a double.

The odds are against slam doubles, too. You will almost never set a slam more than 1 trick, since the opponents have exchanged a great deal of information before they reached their contract. Thus, a double will gain only 50 or 100 points. But when the doubled slam is made, the loss is over 200 points. And very often the enemy will redouble, particularly if some distributional feature, such as a void suit, reassures them; then your loss mounts to 500 or 600 points. So it doesn't pay to double slams simply because you have a hunch that they will go down.

EXAMPLES

Suppose on this auction:

OPENER	YOU	RESPONDER	PARTNER
1 ♠	Pass	2 ♣	Pass
2 ♡	Pass	4 ♡	Pass
6 ♡	?		

you hold:

♠ K Q 10 x x   ♡ J 10 x x   ◊ A Q x   ♣ x

Pass! It looks as though the cards lie wrong for the enemy, but they may be able to withstand the bad splits. The fact that you are so rich in high cards suggests that they are bidding on distribution. Declarer may be void of diamonds; dummy probably has a singleton spade. If you double, you could lose your trump trick. The opponents might even make an overtrick, and then they will surely redouble. Worse still, the opponents could make their contract *because* of your double; then the loss might run into the thousands. It cannot be right to risk all this in order to gain 50 or 100 or even 200 points.

I would not double the slam on the auction above even if I held:

♠ x x x ♡ K Q J ◇ J 10 x x ♣ Q x x

I will surely defeat six hearts, but, warned by my double, the opponents might run to spades or notrump and make *that* contract. This would cost me over a thousand points, and I need too many victories at 50 points each to make up for one such disaster.

Lead-Directing Doubles

Since you do not double slams for penalties, when you think you can beat them, the slam double is an "idle" bid and can be given a special meaning. It says to partner, "I have a fighting chance to set this contract if you get off to a specific, rather unusual, opening lead."

What lead does the double call for? The order of preference is this:

(1) The first side suit (not trumps) bid by dummy.

(2) If dummy has not bid a side suit, then the first side suit bid by declarer.

(3) If neither opponent has bid a side suit but doubler *has* bid a suit of his own, then one of the two unbid suits, *definitely not doubler's bid suit.*

EXAMPLES

Let us see how this works in a few example auctions.

(a) OPENER	PARTNER	RESPONDER	YOU
1 ♠	Pass	2 ◇	Pass
2 ♡	Pass	3 ♣	Pass
4 ♠	Pass	6 ♠	*Double*

This double demands that partner lead diamonds, dummy's first bid suit. To double, you might hold:

♠ x x ♡ x x x x ◇ A Q x ♣ J x x x

Without your lead-directing double, partner would almost surely open a club or a heart, and declarer might well be able to discard any losing diamonds. However, when partner leads diamonds, you have an excellent chance to defeat the slam.

(b) OPENER	PARTNER	RESPONDER	YOU
1 ♡	Pass	3 ♡	Pass
4 ♣	Pass	4 ♡	Pass
6 ♡	Pass	Pass	*Double*

Since dummy has bid no side suit, your double calls for a club lead, declarer's first-bid side suit. For this auction, you might have:

♠ J x x x x 　 ♡ x x 　 ◇ x x x 　 ♣ A K x

It sounds as though opener is trying to stop a club lead with a false cue-bid, and he will succeed unless you double; partner will probably open spades or diamonds unless you direct his lead.

(c) OPENER	PARTNER	RESPONDER	YOU
1 ♡	Pass	4 ♡	4 ♠
6 ♡	Pass	Pass	*Double*

Here no side suit has been bid by either opponent, so your double tells partner not to lead your suit, spades, but to guess between clubs and diamonds. Your hand could be:

♠ A Q J x x x 　 ♡ x x 　 ◇ Q x x x x 　 ♣ Void

You hope that partner will lead clubs (his probable length there should recommend this lead to him) and that the ruff and your ace will defeat the contract.

Observe that in none of these examples are you sure of setting the contract you double. Why do not the heavy odds against slam doubles discourage you here? Because you are not trying to pick up an extra 50 or 100 points by increasing the set. These doubles may gain thousands of points, for without them you are unlikely to defeat the slam at all! If a slam makes despite your lead-directing double, you will have lost from 200 to 700 points extra, according to whether the opponents redouble or make an overtrick. But when a slam is set *because you doubled,* your profit ranges from 1100 to 1600 points. So even if you defeat only one of the three example hands by directing an unusual lead, you will be handsomely ahead. And you figure to do better than that.

DOUBLING THREE NOTRUMP

When Your Side Has Been Silent

The most common reason for doubling an enemy game contract is that the trumps are breaking badly. But what if you double three notrump? More often than not, this is done to demand a specific opening lead. Suppose the auction goes:

OPENER	PARTNER	RESPONDER	YOU
1 ♡	Pass	1 ♠	Pass
1 NT	Pass	3 NT	*Double*

On the surface, your double seems impossible. The enemy auction is not limited (they could have as many as 31 points), so you cannot be doubling speculatively, counting on partner to have a fair hand. You must expect to defeat the contract in your own hand; but if you are so strong, why weren't you in the auction?

The only possible answer is that you have a powerful hand, but passed over one spade because you were long in spades; your suit was bid ahead of you, so you could neither overcall nor double for takeout. Your hand might be:

♠ K Q J 9 x   ♡ A x   ◊ K x x x   ♣ x x

Your double commands partner to lead spades, the first suit bid by dummy. Only if he is void is partner allowed to lead any other suit, and even then he should be apologetic.

The situation is slightly different if you double three

notrump after the sort of enemy bidding sequence that begs to be doubled:

OPENER	PARTNER	RESPONDER	YOU
1 ♠	Pass	2 ◇	Pass
2 ♠	Pass	3 ◇	Pass
3 NT	Pass	Pass	*Double*

Here you are doubling because the opponents cannot afford bad luck, but are getting it. If your hand is:

♠ x   ♡ K 10 x   ◇ K J 9 x   ♣ Q J x x x

you should double, knowing that the breaks are foul for the enemy. On this limited auction, your action is almost surely predicated on diamond strength behind dummy's suit, but does not necessarily call for partner to *lead* diamonds. Obviously, you are prepared for this lead, but you would just as soon have him open a long side suit of his own. You doubled in order to increase the set, not to direct the opening lead.

When You Have Been in the Auction

When your side has been in the auction, your doubles of three notrump once again demand specific leads. If partner has bid a suit:

OPENER	PARTNER	RESPONDER	YOU
1 ◇	2 ♣	2 ◇	Pass
2 NT	Pass	3 NT	*Double*

your double insists that he lead his own suit, undeterred by the opponents' bidding. You have club strength, and do not want partner to try to surprise the enemy by leading an unbid suit.

Similarly, if *you* have bid a suit but partner has not:

OPENER	PARTNER	RESPONDER	YOU
1 ◇	Pass	1 ♠	2 ♡
Double	Pass	3 ◇	Pass
3 NT	Pass	Pass	*Double*

your double commands the lead of your suit. Of course, partner should normally lead your suit anyway, but sometimes he gets ideas of his own. When you double, this is absolutely forbidden. Partner's failure to lead your suit when you double three notrump is justification for homicide in most states of the union. But be merciful if his opening defeats the contract anyway.

9

NEW IDEAS IN
COMPETITIVE BIDDING

♠ ♡ ◇ ♣

Contract bridge is a growing game, and each year has its crop of innovations. Many of the new ideas in the field of competitive bidding merit serious consideration even though they have not yet become standard practice. This chapter presents a sampling of them.

1. THE RESPONSIVE DOUBLE

The "responsive double," a device suggested many years ago by Dr. F. Fielding Reid, is a specialized reply to partner's takeout double after a preemptive raise has intervened. In this sequence:

OPENER	PARTNER	RESPONDER	YOU
1 ♡	Double	2 ♡	*Double*

your double, in standard bidding methods, is for penalties. However, if you use this device, the second double is not for penalties at all, but asks partner to bid his best suit; it is a takeout double in answer to a takeout double—a "responsive" double.

Requirements

A typical hand for the responsive double on the auction above would be:

♠ Q x x   ♡ x x x   ◊ J x x x   ♣ A Q x

You certainly want to enter the auction after partner doubles one heart, but what can you bid over the preemptive raise? Three diamonds is not appealing on such a scrawny suit; you dare not bid notrump without a stopper, you simply have no good action available. That is, you haven't unless you use this new gadget. It is ideal if you can double to show scattered strength and ask partner to take out into *his* best suit (or into notrump if *he* has a stopper). The responsive double neatly handles occasional nasty problems of this sort.

For your double to be responsive, partner must have doubled an opening bid or response for takeout, and your right-hand opponent must have raised the suit that partner doubled. If he has bid a *new* suit:

OPENER	PARTNER	RESPONDER	YOU
1 ♠	Double	2 ♡	Double

your double is for penalties. You can make a responsive double only *directly in response to a takeout double, when a raise (or jump raise under game) intervenes.*

What are the point-count requirements? This depends upon the level at which you force partner to act. On this auction:

OPENER	PARTNER	RESPONDER	YOU
1 ♣	Double	2 ♣	Double

partner can surely bid his best suit at the two-level, so you may have as little as 6 or 7 points. However, for:

OPENER	PARTNER	RESPONDER	YOU
1 ◇	Double	3 ◇	Double

you should have at least 8 or 9 points, since partner must now bid at the three-level. And to double three *spades* on a similar auction, you would need more strength still.

Even if you meet the point-count requirements, you should not use the responsive double when it is unnecessary—when you have a respectable suit of your own to suggest as trumps. For example:

OPENER	PARTNER	RESPONDER	YOU
1 ♡	Double	3 ♡	?

You hold:

♠ J x x x x   ♡ x x   ◇ A Q x   ♣ J x x

Bid three spades. Partner has asked you to bid a suit, and you should not throw this request back to him with a double when you have a suit you can bid yourself.

Development of the Auction

How does the auction proceed after you have made a responsive double and partner, who doubled for takeout originally, has bid his best suit in reply?

OPENER	PARTNER	RESPONDER	YOU
1 ♡	Double	2 ♡	Double
Pass	2 ♠	Pass	?

If you have a few points more than you needed for your double, you can try for game by raising or by bidding a suit of your own. (A new suit bid—for instance, three clubs on the auction above—promises length in *both* unbid suits; with only one suit worth bidding, you would not have used a responsive double.) Most often, though, you have minimum strength and pass partner's response. You have shown your values by doubling, and it is up to partner to try for game if *he* has extra strength.

Partner, with a husky double, should jump in any strong

suit in order to reach game. With enough strength to guarantee game but lacking a good suit to bid (or a stopper to let him jump in notrump), partner can cue-bid the enemy suit, throwing the ball back to you once again.

OPENER	PARTNER	RESPONDER	YOU
1 ◊	Double	2 ◊	Double
Pass	3 ◊		

The partnership is now committed to game, and can search out its maximum contract at leisure.

After Partner Overcalls

Some players use the responsive double as a specialized reply to an *overcall* as well. Then, on this auction:

OPENER	PARTNER	RESPONDER	YOU
1 ◊	1 ♠	2 ◊	Double

your double asks partner to take out into either hearts or clubs, the two unbid suits. He must beware of rebidding his own suit unless it is particularly powerful, for your double denies support for partner. Thus, if partner has overcalled a one-diamond opening with one spade, holding:

♠ A Q x x x   ♡ K 10 x   ◊ A x x   ♣ x x

and you double a two-diamond free response, partner must not pass (your double is for takeout) or rebid spades (you would have raised, not doubled, with spade support). He should bid *two hearts,* taking a preference between your two suits. He expects you to hold a hand like:

♠ x   ♡ J x x x x   ◊ x x   ♣ A Q x x x

That is, you should have length in both unbid suits (at least four cards, usually five) and enough high-card values for a response at the required level. If you hold the hand above, you should *pass* partner's two-heart reply. (Do not become exuberant when partner "bids" one of your suits

—all you have heard is an echo of your own voice.) With a little extra strength, you could raise to three hearts, trying for game.

If *partner* has the extra values, he can make a jump response to your takeout double—usually a jump preference for one of your suits, occasionally a jump in his own suit or in notrump. Alternatively, he may cue-bid the enemy suit to force to game and to allow careful exploration for the proper declaration.

Evaluation of Responsive Doubles

In assessing the worth of any conventional device, three factors must be considered.

First, how well does it do the job it is built for—does it work? (In evaluating "Blackwood," for example, does it keep you out of slams when you are missing two aces? The answer here is that Blackwood usually works well, but occasionally runs into trouble when the trump suit is clubs.)

Second, is it important and necessary, or does it deal with rare situations which can be handled otherwise? (Do you often need to ask for aces? Is there any other way to get this information?)

Third, what price are you paying; what natural bid must be given up to use the device? (How often will you want to bid four notrump naturally, rather than to ask for aces?) The Blackwood Convention passes these tests rather well; what about responsive doubles?

In my experience, the responsive double works well when it is used. It is a simple device, with little scope for gross error by either partner (unless one of you forgets that you are using it).

Is it necessary? Here, I have doubts. If partner's original double promises support for all unbid suits, you can almost always respond by bidding your own long suit, however weak. There *can* be an awkward position, in which you would like to make a takeout bid of your own, but this is so rare that you can play hundreds of deals without seeing a responsive double. This convention is much more necessary to old-fashioned defensive bidders whose partners will double for takeout without the required pattern.

What does it cost? You must give up the penalty double of the preemptive raise. On this auction:

OPENER	PARTNER	RESPONDER	YOU
1 ◊	Double	3 ◊	?

you will once in a long while want to make a business double. Remember, partner is short in diamonds, so you may be quite long. And responder has a weak hand.

My mild objections to the responsive double do not apply to its use after partner *overcalls*. Here:

OPENER	PARTNER	RESPONDER	YOU
1 ◊	1 ♡	3 ◊	?

you cannot happily charge into the auction by bidding one of your suits, since partner has not the promised support, so the conventional double is more necessary. And you will just about never want to double for penalties, since responder's raises after an *overcall* are usually strength-showing, not preemptive; so the price you pay is much lower.

Therefore, I myself prefer to play responsive doubles when partner overcalls and not when he doubles. However, if my partner has firm views to the contrary—not to use them at all, or to use them in all positions—I am willing to go along.

2. THE MICHAELS CUE-BID

The cue-bid of the enemy suit directly over an opening bid has severely limited utility, for it is seldom that you can force to game in the teeth of an opponent's opening. Cannot a sequence like:

OPENER	YOU
1 ◊	2 ◊

be given some real work to do? The most popular new treatment for this cue-bid was suggested by Mike Michaels.

Distribution and Strength Required

The Michaels cue-bid is a forcing but weak takeout, denying the high-card values for a normal takeout *double*, but promising strong distributional values. Many players use this device to show good support for all three unbid suits. For example, with:

♠ Q 10 x x   ♡ K x x x   ◊ K x x x x   ♣ Void

they bid two clubs over a one-club opening. Holding:

♠ K J x x   ♡ x   ◊ A x x x   ♣ J 10 x x

they bid two hearts over a one-heart opening. The primary purpose is to reserve the takeout double for hands which have high-card defensive values, using the cue-bid for distributional, strictly offensive hands.

Another school uses the Michaels cue-bid differently— for *two*-suited, not three-suited hands. Here, the cue-bid over a minor opening promises spades and hearts, ideally five cards of each, but at least four. Holding:

♠ Q 10 x x x   ♡ K J x x x   ◊ x x   ♣ x

they bid two clubs over a one-club opening or two diamonds over one diamond. Note that partner is not invited to respond in the unbid minor suit, but should rather show three-card support for hearts or spades. This treatment can be thought of as "Landy" over a minor suit opening instead of over one notrump.

The cue-bid in a major suit is also a two-suiter—five

cards in the unbid major and five of either diamonds or clubs. Bid two hearts over one heart holding:

♠ Q 10 x x x   ♡ x x   ◇ x   ♣ A Q 10 x x

(Partner can bid spades himself, or can bid notrump to ask you to take out into your minor suit.)

No matter which way you use the Michaels cue-bid, three-suiter or two-suiter, it is essentially a preemptive device. You should not have more than 10 points in high cards, certainly not more than 2 Quick Tricks. And once you have cue-bid, all further action must be taken by *partner*. As with all preemptive bids, the preemptor must not himself take a later sacrifice; he has already shown his hand and partner is in control.

Responding to Michaels Cue-Bid

In responding to partner's cue-bid, you behave much as if he had used a jump overcall or an unusual notrump overcall; that is, you bid at once as high as you are willing to go. For example, you hold:

♠ A J x x x   ♡ 10 x x x   ◇ x x   ♣ x x

With no one vulnerable, the auction goes:

OPENER	PARTNER	RESPONDER	YOU
1 ♡	2 ♡	Double	?

Bid four spades. You should be unwilling to allow the enemy to play four hearts, since partner is weak. Take your sacrifice immediately, before the opponents can exchange information. Conceivably, you might make your contract; in any event, the premature sacrifice gives you your best chance of pushing the opponents beyond their depth.

If, on the same auction, you hold instead:

♠ A J x   ♡ Q J 9 x   ◇ K x x   ♣ Q x x

Bid two spades. You do not wish to go any higher than

this (and partner is not allowed to), since partner is weak and the enemy cannot make much of anything. Two spades should be safe, since you are supporting partner's suit.

Non-vulnerable against vulnerable opponents, you hold:

♠ K Q x x   ♡ Q x   ◇ 10 x x x   ♣ x x x

The auction goes:

OPENER	PARTNER	RESPONDER	YOU
1 ♣	2 ♣	2 NT	?

Jump to four spades. The enemy can probably make virtually any game they bid, so take an anticipatory sacrifice and disrupt their communications. Your hand fits so well with partner's that it is dangerous; the opponents must have a good fit as well.

Evaluation of Michaels Cue-Bid

Personally, I do not like to use the three-suit treatment of the Michaels cue-bid. This works rather well on hands in which partner takes a sacrifice, but most often the opponents buy the contract. Now you have told declarer how to play his cards—what your distribution is, how many honors you hold. The three-suited pattern is handled perfectly well by a takeout double. And if the enemy play the hand, declarer knows less about your point-count and distribution.

There is more to be said for using the cue-bid for two-suiters. Here, there is much more likelihood that your side will find a sacrifice. And weak two-suiters are not easily handled by any other method. Against this, you must set the fact that the perfect hand for a Michaels cue-bid occurs very seldom; you must have just the right pattern and just the right strength, and somehow you never seem to hold it.

For this reason, I do not recommend the device. To use

it, you must give up the cue-bid on strong hands. True, this is very rare also. But the big hands are hard to handle in any other way, and are of extreme importance when they do come up. Therefore, I am reluctant to abandon the big cue-bid for a device of such limited utility.

3. RIPSTRA OVER ONE-NOTRUMP OPENINGS

Two new conventions for defense against weak or normal notrump openings have gained popularity. One of them was developed by J. G. Ripstra.

If you use "Ripstra," *both* minor-suit overcalls (two clubs or two diamonds) of a one-notrump opening ask partner to take out into a major suit. However, the overcall is not completely artificial since you bid your *longer* minor. Thus, with:

♠ A Q x x x   ♡ K J x x   ◇ K x x   ♣ x

you bid two diamonds over one notrump. And with:

♠ K Q x x   ♡ A 10 x x   ◇ x   ♣ A J x x

you bid two clubs. Each of these overcalls invites partner to show support for a major suit. However, partner is permitted to pass when long in the minor suit you have bid, since your overcall promises support for that suit.

Requirements

The point-count requirements for a Ripstra overcall vary according to the distributional pattern of your hand and the size of the enemy notrump. With 4-4-3-2 distribution (two four-card majors), you should have at least 14 high-card points to bid over a strong notrump opening, at least 11 points over a weak notrump. With a singleton or void in one minor suit, you can lower the requirements by 2 or 3 points.

To use this convention, you should have at least four

cards in each major suit (exceptionally, you might use the takeout over a weak notrump with maximum values and only three cards in one of the majors). And it is very dangerous to bid two clubs or two diamonds, Ripstra, without at least three cards in your minor.

Responses

How do you respond to partner's two-club or two-diamond takeout? Unless you have game ambitions, choose your response on the following order of priority. First, bid a four-card or longer major suit if you have one. On rare occasions, bid a strong *three*-card major if no ideal response is available. Second, pass or raise partner's minor suit if you hold four cards or more. (The raise tends to show *five* cards and about 10 points.) Third, respond in the unbid minor suit when you are willing to play opposite partner's probable singleton.

The *jump* response in a major suit invites partner to go on to game unless he holds bare minimum values. You should have at least four cards in your major and at least 11 points in fitting high cards and distribution. If you have game ambitions but no clear idea of where to play, respond two notrump. This is a forcing cue-bid and allows partner to probe for the best suit at the three-level.

Mr. J. G. Ripstra recommends that his convention be used against *weak* one-notrump openings only in the direct position. That is, after one notrump (weak), pass, pass, a reopening overcall of two clubs or two diamonds is natural, not a takeout bid. The reopening *double* asks for a major-suit takeout (but, of course, may be passed for penalties on suitable hands).

Evaluation of Ripstra

This defense against one notrump openings works very well when the takeout bidder holds one of the ideal patterns (5-5-3 or 5-5-4 or 5-4-3-1 or 4-4-4-1). Responder can usually select an excellent contract, for he has three suits to choose among, and his knowledge of partner's likely singleton in the unbid minor helps him value his high cards and distribution exactly. However, Ripstra does not work so well when the takeout bidder holds a *two-suiter* in the majors (5-4-2-2 or 5-5-2-1). Now he has three unpleasant choices: bid a two-card minor, overcall in a five-card major, or pass. Obviously, all three options have glaring flaws.

I consider it important to have some artificial takeout bid for majors over an enemy notrump opening, but it is not necessary to use Ripstra; the Landy Convention (see Chapter 7) is quite satisfactory. However, which is preferable? Certainly, I would rather be playing Ripstra when I hold a three-suited pattern. If partner has no support for the majors we are less likely to suffer a disaster using Ripstra; and if he *has* support, he can value his cards more accurately. Equally, I would rather be playing Landy when I have length only in major suits for now Ripstra might lead to trouble. However, it usually does not cost to bid a two-card minor in Ripstra, since partner tends to respond in a major. And Landy most often works reasonably well on three-suiters, since the real partnership interest is in finding a *major* suit fit. Finally, the three-suit pattern is more common than the more freakish two-suit pattern; this argues for Ripstra. But the freak two-suiter is more likely to yield a big profit for your side—this argues for Landy.

Obviously, the choice is not clear-cut. My personal opinion is that Ripstra has a slight advantage but that you should use Landy. Why? Because it costs less. To use Ripstra, you must give up two natural overcalls, two clubs *and* two diamonds. Landy is very nearly as effective and you pay only half the price.

3. ASTRO OVER ONE-NOTRUMP OPENINGS

The latest and most complicated device for defense against one-notrump openings is called "Astro" after its originators, Paul Allinger, Roger Stern, and Lawrence Rosler. It, too, uses both minor suit overcalls, two clubs and two diamonds, as artificial takeout bids. However, each overcall promises length in only *one* major suit, not in *both* majors as in Landy or Ripstra.

Distribution, Strength Required

To use Astro, you must have a two-suited hand (at least 5-4) with four cards or more in one of the majors. The two diamond overcall promises four or five *spades* (and some other suit, not necessarily diamonds). The two club overcall promises four or five *hearts* (and some minor suit as well—not a side *spade* suit since you did not overcall two diamonds). Thus, you might overcall *two diamonds* after a one-notrump opening holding any of these hands:

♠ A Q x x	♡ x	◇ x x	♣ A Q 10 x x x
♠ K 10 x x	♡ K Q x x x	◇ x x	♣ A x
♠ Q J x x x	♡ x	◇ A K x x x	♣ x x

You could overcall *two clubs* with either:

♠ x x	♡ K J x x	◇ A K J x x	♣ x x
♠ x	♡ A Q 10 x x	◇ Q x x	♣ K J 10 x

The distributional requirements for an Astro takeout are (1) a four– or five-card major suit (not six cards, for then you would overcall or double) and (2) a four–, five–, or six-card side suit. You must have at least nine cards in your two suits.

The strength requirements vary somewhat according to vulnerability and position, but are not much affected by the size of the enemy notrump. To act directly over the opening, you should have close to an opening bid yourself with 2 Quick Tricks at least; seldom less than 10 or 11 points in high cards, and usually more. However, in the *reopening* position, particularly non-vulnerable, you may use an Astro takeout on little more than favorable distribution and high spirits; partner is marked for high cards if you do not have them.

Responding to Astro

There are two likely responses to partner's Astro takeout. One is the bid of the major suit he has promised, his "anchor" suit—hearts if he has overcalled two clubs, spades, if he has overcalled two diamonds. You should respond in the anchor suit whenever you hold four cards in it and have no great desire to reach game. With:

♠ J x x   ♡ J x x   ◇ K x x   ♣ Q x

bid two hearts if partner overcalls two clubs; bid two spades if he overcalls two diamonds. You may support partner's announced major suit even with only three cards if you have some values for play there.

Thus, with:

♠ A J x   ♡ Q x x   ◇ x   ♣ 10 x x x x x

bid two spades in response to two diamonds, or two hearts over two clubs.

If you cannot support the anchor major, your most common response is to bid the next higher suit over partner's takeout—two hearts over two diamonds, or two diamonds over two clubs. This may be done with only two or three cards in that suit; partner will not pass unless this is his five-card suit. For example, with:

♠ x x x   ♡ x x ◇ J x x   ♣ K 10 x x x

you should respond two diamonds to two clubs, or two hearts to two diamonds. (You *could* bid two spades in answer to two diamonds, but should avoid supporting partner's major suit with three cards and scanty values.)

There are other responses possible with poor hands. If

you hold six cards or more in the minor suit partner has bid, you may pass a hopeless hand. And you may bid the fourth suit (two spades over two clubs; three clubs over two diamonds) with a strong six– or seven-card holding. This action should be avoided unless your suit or strength provide security; it gets the auction up rather high, and partner may bid still higher if he has maximum values. Holding:

♠ x x   ♡ x x   ◊ Q x   ♣ J 10 9 x x x x

pass if partner bids two clubs, but respond two hearts to two diamonds—do not bid three clubs with so weak a hand.

Once in a while, you will have game ambitions after partner uses Astro (particularly if the opponents use weak notrump openings). You can jump to game in the anchor major with four-card support and 12 or 13 points. With 10 to 12 points, you can invite game with a jump to three of partner's major (of course, with at least four-card support). When you have a hand with game possibilities but only three cards in partner's announced major, you can "cuebid" two notrump. Partner will now "rebid" his major if it is a five-carder, jumping to game with maximum values; if partner has only a four-card major, he will show his side long suit. Thus, if you hold:

♠ A 10 x x   ♡ K x x   ◊ K J x x   ♣ x x

bid three spades in answer to two diamonds, or two notrump in reply to two clubs.

Further Development of the Auction

How do you proceed after partner responds to your Astro takeout? If he has supported your announced major, you will pass unless you have substantial extra values. With a maximum, you can raise to three in the anchor suit (but you must have five-card length; remember, partner may have only three cards) or bid your long side suit at the three-level. Suppose you have bid two clubs over a one notrump opening and partner has responded two hearts. What is your rebid with:

(a) ♠ x x   ♡ A Q x x   ◊ A Q x x x   ♣ x x
(b) ♠ x   ♡ K J x x x   ◊ A K 10 x x   ♣ K x
(c) ♠ A x   ♡ A J x x   ◊ K Q 10 x x x   ♣ x

Holding hand (a), *pass.* Game is inconceivable since partner did not jump in response, and even two hearts may be in great jeopardy. Holding hand (b), raise to *three hearts* showing a five-card suit and inviting game. Holding hand (c), try for game by bidding *three diamonds;* this denies a five-card heart suit.

When partner's response to Astro is in the next higher suit, the "denial" suit, show your longest suit. If this is the denial suit, pass; if this is your announced major, "rebid" it; if this is a new suit, bid it now. Holding:

♠ x x   ♡ K J x x x   ◊ K Q x x   ♣ K x

you overcall two clubs, and partner responds two diamonds. Rebid *two hearts.* If your red suits were reversed, you would pass two diamonds. Observe that if you held, instead:

♠ x x   ♡ K Q x x   ◊ K x   ♣ K J x x x

you would be compelled to bid three clubs over the two-diamond reply. Since you hate to gallop up to the three-level on such a poor suit, you should not have used Astro—it is wiser to pass rather than risk the overcall. Always plan your rebid over the expected denial response of the next higher suit.

There are two other rare rebids which you may make after using an Astro takeout. One is to bid spades after you have denied holding four spades by using the two club takeout. If you hold:

♠ A Q x   ♡ K J x x   ◊ x   ♣ A Q x x x

bid two clubs over one notrump; when partner replies two diamonds, rebid two spades. Partner knows that you have only three, and will look for a better suit (by bidding two notrump) unless *he* is long.

The other unusual rebid, two notrump, also shows three-suited pattern—here, your major and *both* minors. For example, holding:

♠ K Q x x   ♡ Void   ◇ A J x x x   ♣ A K J x

bid two diamonds for takeout, and rebid two notrump over either a two-heart or two-spade reply. Partner will know that you have only four spades, that you have extra strength, that you have tolerance for both minor suits.

This is the second occasion in which we have seen a cue-bid of two notrump in an Astro sequence. Two notrump, bid by either partner at virtually any stage, is forcing—asking partner to clarify his strength or distribution. It does not necessarily indicate game ambitions; its most frequent use is as responder's rebid when he wants to play in the takeout bidder's second suit. For example:

	PARTNER		YOU
	♠ x x		♠ J x x x
	♡ A K x x x		♡ x
	◇ A J x x		◇ Q x x x
	♣ Q x		♣ K x x x

OPENER	PARTNER	RESPONDER	YOU
1 NT	2 ♣	Pass	2 ◇
Pass	2 ♡	Pass	2 NT

Here, you bid two notrump at your second turn secure in the knowledge that partner has a four-card minor. (He cannot have four *spades* when he bids two clubs for takeout.) Partner will bid three diamonds and you will pass.

Evaluation of Astro

It is too early to judge how well Astro works. So far, very few of the top experts have adopted it, and the convention is too complicated for general popularity. Thus, Astro has not been tested extensively in competition.

Its great theoretical advantage is that it allows relatively safe and accurate competition against one notrump openings with *any* two-suited pattern. Landy and Ripstra can be used only with both major suits, while Astro can be used with one major and a minor, *or* with both majors. It is irritating to hear one notrump opened on your right when you hold:

♠ x   ♡ Q 10 x x   ◇ A 10 x x x   ♣ A K J

Unless you use Astro, you cannot enter the auction intelligently. Yet the hand may well belong to your side, even for a game.

However, there are theoretical objections to Astro. On the vast majority of hands, either both sides have a good suit fit or neither has. On a misfit hand, you will obviously be better off to let the enemy play one notrump; and on a good fitting hand, you are likely to be out-bid if you compete. After all, you would probably *double* one notrump holding as many or more points than opener; and when you hold fewer, you are at a disadvantage. The argument for Landy and Ripstra is that this disadvantage is mitigated when you hold *both* majors. On good-fitting hands, the enemy suit is a minor while yours is a major, so you can compete effectively. And if your competition jostles them out of notrump into a suit, it is into a low-scoring club or diamond contract.

What is more, the spade-heart two-suiter—clearly the most important one—is the pattern which Astro handles worst. When you bid two diamonds and partner replies two hearts, you know next to nothing about his heart holding; he could have two little or five to the ace-queen. If you have five hearts yourself, you will pass, and may miss game. If you have five spades and four hearts, you will bid two spades, and partner may pass with two spades and five hearts, fearing that your side suit is a minor. Thus, it is difficult to find a fit in hearts just when it is most rewarding to do so—when you hold spades and you cannot be outbid easily.

My final objection to Astro is the same one I had to Ripstra; it uses two artificial bids where Landy uses one. It is not often that you want to overcall one notrump with a minor suit, but nothing comes up often in bridge, and it is annoying not to be able to make a natural club or diamond bid when you do hold the hand which calls for it. Obviously, this will happen twice as often when you use both minors for takeout.

Despite the flaws I find in Astro, I have a sneaking admiration for the device; it is well worked out, and handles many distributional patterns which create insoluble problems in any other method. Some variation of this convention may conceivably come to be regarded as the best defense against one-notrump openings. Perhaps the solution lies in the direction of ignoring heart-club or heart-diamond two suiters, and using two clubs for both majors, two diamonds for spades and a side minor.

4. WEISS OVER PREEMPTIVE OPENINGS

In Chapter 6, several artificial devices for defense against preemptive openings—Fishbein, cheaper minor, etc.—were examined. These are designed to allow a penalty double over a shut-out bid, with some special overcall reserved as a conventional takeout for unbid suits. Recently, Larry Weiss of Los Angeles has suggested combining a conventional bid for takeout with an *optional*—not a penalty—double.

Double, Takeout, or Pass

A typical "Weiss" double of an enemy opening three-heart bid would look like:

♠ 10 x x   ♡ K 10 x   ◇ A Q 10 x   ♣ A K x

This hand requires action, but is suited to neither a takeout nor to a penalty double. If partner has a long suit and offensive distribution, he will take out your "Weiss" double, confident of finding you with the honor cards to support a high contract. And if partner's distribution is more balanced, he will pass your double, counting on you for substantial defensive strength.

In contrast, a hand like this one:

♠ A Q x x   ♡ x   ◊ K J x x   ♣ A J x x

is *not* a "Weiss" double of an opening three-heart bid. Here, you want partner to take out even into a four-card suit. Thus, you bid four clubs over three hearts, the cheaper minor used as an artificial takeout device.

Finally, if your right-hand opponent bids three hearts when you hold:

♠ x x   ♡ K J 10 x x   ◊ A Q J x   ♣ x x

you must pass, not double. Here, partner is almost sure to have an unbalanced hand with an attractive black suit, and will exercise his option to take out your double. Then you will get a minus instead of a plus, for you do not have the high card strength to support partner's contract.

Evaluation of "Weiss"

The "Weiss" double works admirably on the hands for which it is suited; it is a flexible partnership tool. However, the cheaper minor takeout is less successful. It wastes bidding space over three-heart and three-diamond openings, and it forces one player to make a decision for his partnership when he holds a slightly unbalanced hand over a preemptive opening: he must double or use the takeout when either could be wrong.

To use "Weiss," you must give up the takeout double. Personally, I find that this is too heavy a price to pay. However, if you are already addicted to an artificial take-

out like "cheaper minor" or "Fishbein," you will probably do well to substitute the *optional* for the strictly
penalty double.

One reasonable compromise is to use "Weiss" over black
suits and takeout doubles over red suits. But only if you
and partner have good memories!

5. CUE-BID RESPONSES TO OVERCALLS

The General Purpose Cue-Bid

Several modern expert partnerships have adopted a
method of responding to overcalls similar to their responses to doubles: the cue-bid is the only force. Then, on
this auction:

OPENER	PARTNER	RESPONDER	YOU
1 ♡	1 ♠	Pass	2 ♡

your two-heart bid is the only really strong action available. If, instead, you had bid (or even jumped in) a new
suit, partner could, and often would, pass. If you had
jump-raised to three spades, it would be preemptive, not
invitational to game; you would have cue-bid and raised
spades next to suggest game. You would employ the auction above with any of these hands:

♠ K x x	♡ x x	◇ A Q x x	♣ J x x x
♠ K J x x	♡ x	◇ A Q x x	♣ K x x x
♠ K x	♡ x x	◇ A K J 10 x x	♣ K x x
♠ x	♡ A K	◇ K Q x x x	♣ K J x x x

This general-purpose cue-bid is not forcing to game.
Partner may pass in a part score contract if you subse-
quently support his suit, or if you bid notrump or if you
rebid a suit of your own. He may *not* pass so long as you
bid new suits.

The principal advantage of this method is that you can

bid a new suit in response to partner's overcall without forcing your side to a high contract. For example, holding:

♠ x   ♡ K J 10 9 x x   ◇ Q x x   ♣ x x x

you can bid:

OPENER	PARTNER	RESPONDER	YOU
1 ♣	1 ♠	Pass	2 ♡

A secondary benefit is that you have available the preemptive jump raise of partner's overcall. You can bid:

OPENER	PARTNER	RESPONDER	YOU
1 ♣	1 ♠	Pass	3 ♠

when you have some horrible hand like:

♠ J x x x   ♡ x   ◇ K x x x x   ♣ x x x

There is little risk to either of these sequences, despite your weakness, for partner knows that you would have cue bid, instead, had you hopes for game.

Evaluation

The normal usage of the cue-bid response—a fit with partner, first-round control of the enemy suit, slam aspirations—is so rare that you are giving up little in adopting the method. And it does allow you to handle certain types of weak hands very well.

However, my feeling is that *strong* hands, the ones that call for the cue-bid response in this style, are not bid so effectively. The cue-bid is too vague; it can carry too many different messages. The proponents of this method maintain that the subsequent auction will always resolve the ambiguity, but the fact is that confusion can develop. This is particularly true when opener crowds the auction:

OPENER	PARTNER	RESPONDER	YOU
1 ◇	1 ♡	Pass	2 ◇
4 ◇	?		?

Suppose that partner has overcalled with:

♠ A 10 x   ♡ A Q x x x x   ◇ x x x   ♣ x

If your cue-bid conceals a normal jump raise, he wants to bid four hearts. If it is based on a strong single raise, he wants to pass. If you have a spade suit, he must bid four spades; if you have a strong hand with clubs, he would like to double. As it is, partner can do little but pass the buck to you. And how can *you* make an intelligent decision, knowing almost as little about partner's hand as he does about yours?

I would have no objection to giving the cue-bid response a *specific* meaning: a fit with partner's suit with game ambitions, *or* biddable holdings in both missing suits, *or* a willingness to play both in notrump and in partner's suit. But to lump all these meanings (plus a dozen more) into one all-purpose strong bid is to court disaster.

6. ROMAN JUMP OVERCALLS

Requirements

In the "Roman Club" System, the jump overcall is used to show a two-suited hand. The overcaller has the suit he bids plus the *next higher-ranking* unbid suit. Thus, in these sequences:

	OPENER	YOU
(a)	1 ◇	2 ♡
(b)	1 ♣	2 ♠

you would indicate *hearts* plus *spades* in (a); *spades* plus *diamonds* in (b) (clubs, the suit next higher than spades, has been bid).

Notice that you can show any combination of two unbid suits over a suit opening. Suppose the opening is one heart. With spades-clubs, you bid two spades; with clubs-diamonds, you bid three clubs; with spades-diamonds, you bid three diamonds.

What are the requirements for this jump overcall? You should have at least ten cards in your two suits, normally five of each; exceptionally, you might hold six cards in the suit you bid, four cards in the next higher. The strength required varies with vulnerability and level, but the bid is primarily intended to seek out sacrifices and to interfere with the enemy auction. Like the "unusual no-trump," the Roman jump overcall is fundamentally pre-emptive.

All three hands below are possible Roman jump over-calls of two spades after a one-diamond opening:

(a) ♠ K J 10 x x   ♡ x   ◇ x   ♣ Q 10 9 x x x

(b) ♠ Q 10 x x x x   ♡ K x   ◇ x   ♣ K Q J x

(c) ♠ K Q 10 x x   ♡ x   ◇ x x   ♣ A K J x x

Example (a) would be the typical strength when non-vulnerable against vulnerable opponents; example (b) is normal strength on equal vulnerability; example (c) would be the maximum strength for equal vulnerability, the minimum when vulnerable against non-vulnerable opponents.

The responses to these jump overcalls are very like those to "unusual notrump" overcalls and Michaels cue-bids. With a lack-luster hand, partner takes a preference: passing, or bidding the next higher suit if he greatly prefers it. With strong support for one of your suits, partner jumps at once to the highest contract he can afford.

Evaluation of Roman Jump Overcalls

The two-suited jump overcall gets excellent results when it is used. On good-fitting hands, opener's side is often crowded into inaccurate bidding, while overcaller's side is in perfect comfort. Occasionally a huge gain is forthcoming. The defending side bids and makes game, when the opponents could make game themselves in a suit they have not found. And this device is not costly even on misfit hands. The overcaller would have been tempted to bid both of his suits anyway, and he may well stay lower when he is able to bid both suits at once.

One possible objection is that you rarely hold the proper pattern and strength for this overcall; you use it perhaps once in a hundred deals. However, two-suiters are extremely important hands (both sides can often make high contracts; the swings can be enormous), so perhaps it pays to set aside a bid for them.

The main reason that I do not recommend the Roman jump overcall is that it displaces the one-suited preemptive jump. The weak jump overcall described in Chapter 1 and 5 is essential. If you do not use it, the whole structure of modern defensive bidding, the "pattern" takeout double, the constructive overcall, etc., tumbles to the ground. The price-tag on the two-suited device is much higher than I can afford.

Two-Suited Simple Overcalls

An interesting new idea, suggested by Alan Truscott, is to use two-suited *simple* overcalls to compete over powerful artificial opening bids. Originally, this was a defense against the "Neapolitan Club" System, in which all strong hands, regardless of distribution, are opened one club. Any *non-jump* overcall shows that suit plus the next higher. Thus, over one club:

$$1 \, \Diamond \; = \; \text{diamonds and hearts}$$
$$1 \, \heartsuit \; = \; \text{hearts and spades}$$
$$1 \, \spadesuit \; = \; \text{spades and clubs}$$
$$2 \, \clubsuit \; = \; \text{clubs and diamonds}$$

There are two pairs of non-touching suits: clubs-hearts and diamonds-spades. The *double* of one club shows the pair including clubs (clubs-hearts); the overcall of one no-trump shows the other pair (diamonds-spades).

Obviously, this defense can be used against other systems in which one club is an artificial strength-showing opening bid. And it can be used against the artificial two-club opening, one level higher.

The reasoning behind it is this: to want to compete against a powerful opening bid, you must have a wildly unbalanced hand, either with one very long suit, or with two fairly long ones. You can *jump* overcall with any one-suiter worth bidding at all, so the simple overcall can be reserved to show your specific two-suited pattern.

You can adapt this defense for use against *any* artificial opening bid. If the forcing opening is one diamond or two diamonds (as it is in three new American systems), the suit overcalls are the same but the double shows diamonds-spades, while the notrump overcall is clubs-hearts.

In these days of proliferating artificial systems, you must be prepared to fight back with some fancy gadgets of your own. When your opponents announce that they are playing the "Schenken Club" or the "Big Diamond" or the "Little Major," you need not sit quiet and look impressed. Tell them that you use the Truscott defense against their artificial openings. Probably it will never come up, but you will have made your presence felt at the table.